*Building a Home
for the Heart*

Building a Home
for the Heart

Using Metaphors in Value-Centered Circles

Patricia Thalhuber, B.V.M., & Susan Thompson

Foreword by Kay Pranis
Illustrations by Loretta Draths

Living Justice Press

Building a Home for the Heart

"I must admit that when I first went to the talking Circle at the VOARCC [a corrections center for women], I had no clue about what to expect. I felt lost, scared, and alone. I wanted to leave the Circle before it even began, but when the Circle was opened, I felt safe almost immediately. I felt that maybe I could trust this Circle; maybe here I could talk and let out what I had been holding in since I was arrested. It turned out to be a powerful experience right from the beginning."

· *Circle participant incarcerated at the VOARCC*

Janis (on the left) and Fawn, her daughter

"The Circle helped me stay focused on developing into the woman I am today. It brought things I knew to the surface, like being honest not only with myself but also with others. The Circle involved creativity: we were able to create things with markers to match the value of the Circle. The cards given at the closing of the Circle were practical, and the messages on the cards were close to my heart.

"It was so hard at first when I got out. The trust factor was not there between my daughter and me. Getting back together to renew that trust when she was sixteen was a long road; we had to face a lot of denial. Now she is twenty-one, and we are reunited as mother and daughter."

· *Janis, one of the Circle participants previously incarcerated at the VOARCC*

Living Justice Press
St. Paul, Minnesota 55105

*For information about permission to reproduce selections from this book,
please contact:*
Permissions, Living Justice Press, 2093 Juliet Avenue, St. Paul, MN 55105
Tel. (651) 695-1008 or contact permissions through our
Web site: www.livingjusticepress.org.

Cataloging-in-Publication
(Provided by Quality Books, Inc.)

Thalhuber, Patricia, 1940–
    Building a home for the heart : using metaphors in value-centered
circles / Patricia Thalhuber & Susan Thompson ; foreword by Kay Pranis ;
illustrations by Loretta Draths. — 1st ed.
    p.   cm.
    Includes index.
    LCCN 2006937609
    ISBN 0-9721886-3-0

    1. Interpersonal conflict. 2. Interpersonal communication. 3. Metaphor—
Psychological aspects. 4.Healing circles. I. Thompson, Susan, 1960–
II. Title.

BF637.I48T43   2007   158.2
                          QBI07-600069

    LCCN 2006937609
    ISBN 0-9721886-3-0

Poetry by the Circle participant at the VOARCC is printed with the author's
permission.

"The Ugly Feather" story is excerpted from Kay Pranis, Barry Stuart, and
Mark Wedge, *Peacemaking Circles: From Crime to Community* (2003) and is
reprinted with permission from Living Justice Press.

11 10 09 08 07 5 4 3 2 1
Copyediting by Cathy Broberg
Cover design by David Spohn
Interior design by Wendy Holdman
Composition at Prism Publishing Center, Minneapolis, Minnesota
Printed by Sheridan Books, Ann Arbor, Michigan, on
    Natures Book Recycled paper

Dedication

This guide is dedicated to the Indigenous Peoples of the world whose healing use of the Circle process lives among us, restoring balance and harmony to our planet. This guide is also dedicated to those who use the sacred way of the Circle to bring justice, balance, and harmony to individual and community relationships.

～～

I dedicate these pages to my parents, Clara and Herbert Thalhuber; my brothers, Wayne and James Thalhuber; my sister, Joan Thalhuber; my sister, Margaret Thalhuber, for her editing and guidance throughout this project; as well as to my religious community, the Sisters of Charity of the Blessed Virgin Mary, B.V.M., for their support and belief in a just world.

· *Patricia Thalhuber, B.V.M.*

～～

I dedicate this work to my husband, Jeff Thompson, whose love and support allow me to feel safe and warm; to my daughter, Amelia Thompson, who teaches me about living in the present; to my first child, Katie Josephson, who taught me about allowing the grand potential of tough situations to emerge; and to my parents, Donna and Duane Schwalbe, who showed me how to start from where I'm standing.

· *Susan Thompson*

Acknowledgments

We want to thank those who contributed enormously to the creation of this guide: the Circle of Harmony Team—Mark and Maggie Clements and Paula Daine—for their belief in the Circle as a process for healing and reunion; Living Justice Press for their courageous perspective on justice and for "walking their talk"; and the staff and residents at the Volunteers of America Regional Corrections Center in Roseville, Minnesota, for their support and assistance in developing ongoing talking Circles at their center. We thank these people and groups for welcoming us as partners in justice and personal restoration.

We also want to thank community members who proofread the manuscript: Lucy Berry, Gina Birdhorse, Maggie Clements, Mark Clements, Bryan Flemming, Donna Flemming, Emma Geyer, Mary Maas, Donna Schwalbe, Veronica Schwalbe, Carol Spiegel, B.V.M., Lu Taylor, Clara Thalhuber, Margaret Thalhuber, and Teri Twadowski. We are also grateful to Mark LaPointe for sharing his insights, which we have incorporated into this guide.

Kay Pranis has dedicated her life to promoting the use of Circles, and we are deeply grateful to her for reading the manuscript and writing the foreword to help frame our work.

Finally, and with deep humility, we want to acknowledge all our relations and how they bless us with wisdom and guidance.

In Remembrance

Ogiimaa-Anakwat
Curtis Joseph Brown
1961–2004

Dear Self,

I hope sobriety is treating you well;
      you'll only be able to move forward.
Building a little each day on your sobriety
      I know it won't seem like you are
          progressing at times.
Believe you are a person who has much to offer
      and that it's all right to have feelings . . .
      It's how you let those feelings out
      in a good way that matters most!
Always remember who you really are . . .
      and why you are here;
      feel from your heart.

                    —*Curtis Brown*

Contents

Foreword

In writing *Peacemaking Circles: From Crime to Community*, my colleagues and I emphasized the importance of values that nurture and promote good connections to others as the foundation of the Circle process and therefore as the foundation for walking in a good way in the world. In my work since that time, my sense of the importance of conversations about values has deepened. I understood then that values were important, but I did not comprehend how powerful the actual conversations about values could be in helping people access their best selves and in bringing that forward in their relationships with one another. I now believe that conversations about the values that represent our "best self" need to happen over and over again in many different contexts. These values serving as the foundation of our lives function like the roots of a tree. They need to be fed and watered regularly.

Pat Thalhuber and Susan Thompson have written a wonderful book that gives us many ways to feed and water the value root system that we want to hold up our lives. Their book stimulates thinking about the meaning of these core values and describes very specific ways that we can generate dialogue about these values in groups. Conversations about values are not easy to enter into given our daily lives. Deep conversations require a space apart—a place where there is a conscious intent to have respectful speaking and listening. And even when we create that space apart from our daily lives, as in a Circle, we often need prompters to get beyond the clutter of thoughts racing through our heads to the wisdom of the heart and spirit as well.

Pat and Susan have chosen metaphors as a tool to help us

bring our hearts and spirits into dialogue with our heads and with each other. We use language to engage a metaphor, but ultimately metaphors speak to us in images, engaging our intuition and holistic processing. I have found metaphors to be very powerful in my work in Circles. Because images are less dependent on language skills, metaphors have helped me bridge a gap in language among the participants in a Circle. Metaphors often help us express something that we cannot put directly into words. They help make the abstract more concrete so that we can get our arms around it and examine it from many perspectives.

This book presents both a philosophy and a roadmap for bringing that philosophy to life. The philosophy inspires us to values-based living, and it assumes that values-based living is enhanced by intentional conversations about values. The roadmap describes particular pathways that have been successful in engaging a group in dialogue about values in ways that helped participants make constructive changes in their lives. The goal is not just to be able to talk about values. The goal is to connect deeply to our own desire to live those values and then to practice them in our lives outside of Circle. The intentional conversations in Circle strengthen the muscles that help us live the values in all parts of our lives.

While sharing their experiences of creating ways to exercise those muscles among a group of incarcerated women, these two experienced Circle keepers make it clear that there is not a single way to do this. Readers can follow the detailed instructions provided to feel how the process works and to sense the underlying template. Following the template, readers can then use their creativity and life experience to design metaphors that are particularly responsive to their own context.

Together with the women who participated in their Circles at the Volunteers of America Regional Corrections Center, Pat and Susan have made a great contribution to the community by sharing their journey of using Circles to explore and understand the values they want to guide their lives. They have organized that experience into a framework that any of us could use with family, friends, coworkers, or neighbors.

Based on a values exercise I have done with thousands of people across age, culture, socioeconomic status, religion, race, and education differences, I believe that the values discussed in this book are universal. These values are the common ground on which we can come together despite very difficult and painful differences. Consequently, intentional conversations about these values are essential to work out how we can all live with one another in a good way without suppressing our individual differences. These are the critical conversations of our time, and this book is a lovely guide for having those conversations.

Thank you, dear reader, for stepping into this conversation about values.

—Kay Pranis

Introduction:
The Circle Process and Its Uses

Wisdom lies in respecting our conflicts, hurt,
and pain.

For thousands of years, Indigenous Peoples have gathered in
Circles or councils to share stories for the purpose of resolving differences and restoring balance within communities. This
age-old vision of how justice can be restored is now held by a
growing number of people—Native and non-Native—who
wish to elevate their obligations to each other and seek resolutions to conflicts on higher ground. Through honorably conducted Circles—talking Circles, peacemaking Circles, support
Circles, healing Circles, family Circles, educational Circles, and
other types of Circles—participants come together to navigate
the challenging terrain of healing harms and working for social
justice. We believe that Circles can help individuals take the first
steps toward personal and communal transformation.

In 2003, Living Justice Press published a book that has quickly
become a core text for this work. *Peacemaking Circles: From Crime
to Community* by Kay Pranis, Barry Stuart, and Mark Wedge describes not only the outer dynamics of the Circle process but also
its inner side, its principles and philosophy, which are rooted in
values. We would like to share two excerpts from this book that
convey what the Circle process can mean for participants:

Circles bring us together to share who we are beyond our appearances. They're places of listening—of hearing what it's like to be someone else. They're also places for being heard—for expressing what's on our minds and hearts and having others receive it deeply. Telling our stories in the safe space of Circles opens windows on each other's lives, giving us moments when we can witness the path another has walked as well as feel that others appreciate our own path. The life stories shared are naturally transforming. Speakers and listeners are touched and changed; so are their relationships. Circles don't "make" this happen; rather they provide a forum—imbued with a philosophy and format that reflects it—where profound change is highly likely to happen. (p. 3)

In Circles, we share who we are in order to begin our healing journeys together. We reveal our wounds, stories, histories, as well as our potentials. The justice we experience, then, is less rule-and-law centered and more human centered. It's a person-oriented, soulful justice—a justice that we both give and receive by respecting each other, expressing care and concern, and working for mutual healing. (p. 14)

Our first experiences with Circles occurred within Native communities. Circles are, after all, Indigenous in origin and common worldwide in one form or another. The vastly disproportionate rate of incarceration of Indigenous people have led many Indigenous communities to use the Circle process with the dominant criminal justice system to help their people. Sometimes an established community Circle program can create alternatives to incarceration, especially for young people. In other cases, Circles support incarcerated individuals when they are released and struggling to re-enter their families and communities.

In our case, we took the Circle process into a women's prison to support women who were "doing time." This guide is a result of that work. It reflects six years of experience in keeping talking Circles at the Volunteers of America Regional Corrections Center (VOARCC) in Roseville, Minnesota. While serving as keepers for these Circles, we used metaphors to encourage Circle participants to discuss the values most important to them. Metaphors, including the ones we describe in this book, proved to be a powerful tool for engaging the residents in sharing their values and in exploring how they might apply them in their lives. With this in mind, we offer our ideas and experiences to those who seek to deepen their exploration of individual and shared values in their Circle processes.

> "I've sat in Circle many times, tapping the ancient roots. Especially at times when we've struggled through an impasse, those roots nourished us with forgiveness, healing, reconciliation, and the deepening of relationships among hurting people."
>
> –Harv Bartz, Circle keeper

Settings for Using This Approach

Although our work developed in this context, the methods we share in this book can be used in virtually any setting, from the most personal to the most public. That's because discussing values is essential to the Circle process. Whenever Circles are held, values are one of the first topics that participants discuss.

The use of Circles is growing largely because of how transformative the process can be. For example, when one family started using Circles to improve relations between the parents and their two sons, one teenage son who seldom spoke around the house became quite vocal and expressive during the Circle. When his father later expressed his surprise, the son replied that he never felt that his family listened to him, so he hadn't seen much point in talking. Spouses familiar with the Circle process also use it to resolve differences as well as to maintain connection in the midst of hectic schedules and child-rearing routines.

Schools and youth centers are more public places where Circles are having powerful and positive effects. Young people seem to respond naturally to the Circle process and quickly embrace it. Circles can help with any number of situations that young people face, from bullying and "discipline" issues to racial and class conflicts to cliques and gangs to student-teacher relations to student violence and suicide. Regular morning Circles where students "check in" often become known as students' favorite period in the daily schedule. Barriers come down, misunderstandings are aired before they cause conflict, and students come to know and appreciate each other and their teachers (those who participate) far more deeply. In the process, students learn how to listen and respect both others and themselves. They develop skills for being together in a good way that will profoundly affect their lives and relationships as they grow up.

Purposes for Convening Circles:
Situation Specific and Ongoing

Using Circles to resolve specific conflicts can be powerful. Circles

+ introduce people to different ways of being together
+ demonstrate that, when people speak from their hearts in a safe, respectful space, amazing things can happen
+ help people experience both others and themselves differently
+ lead to resolutions that most likely would not have occurred through more conventional methods of conflict resolution
+ show that conflicts can be doorways to deep change and healing

+ provide a way for us to respect our conflicts by exploring the messages they carry about ourselves and our
  relationships.

In addition to situation-specific uses of Circles, though, ongoing Circle programs offer a qualitatively different experience.
Using Circles on a regular basis builds
community. It deepens the understanding,
trust, and capacities to share among those
involved. It is also creative, since it is virtually impossible for people to come together in a good way over time and not be
creative.

> "The most mean-
> ingful part of
> Circle is par-
> ticipating in the
> amazing process of
> repairing the harm
> between people."
>
> –Mark LaPointe,
> Circle steward

In his 1972 classic book, *Pedagogy of
the Oppressed*, Paolo Freire argues powerfully that learning to communicate human-
to-human, heart-to-heart—in his words,
engaging each other as "Subjects" instead
of objects—forms the foundation of authentic social change. The
kind of dialogue that ongoing Circles exemplify is revolutionary
by its very nature, because domination and hierarchy have no
place in it. We listen as equals and speak as equals, each person remaining open and humble in a shared search for truth and justice.
As we discuss in the next section, Freire contends that such revolutionary dialogue absolutely requires that we practice our best
values—precisely those that Circles imbibe.

It is within these ongoing Circle programs that the experiences we share in this book might be most useful.

How This Book Might Be Used

We have written this book to be used as a support to those involved with Circles. As such, it is not a book that has to be read
cover to cover. It rather suggests a framework for exploring values

in Circles—a template for value-based Circle dialogues that can be adapted in many ways.

For those new to Circles, we refer readers to the book *Peacemaking Circles* for a more thorough treatment of the Circle process. In a later section, though, we do offer a brief overview of some of the most basic elements of Circles, including the meaning of key terms, such as "keeper," "talking piece," or "pass" (see pp. 41–48).

This book is divided into two parts.

Part 1, *Using Metaphors to Explore Values in Circles*, presents our overall approach—why it is so important to clarify our values, how metaphors help us do this, and how we arrived at this approach. We also share some of our experiences with using metaphors in Circles, illustrating how metaphors can open us to deeper dialogues about the values we most want to live.

Part 2, *Sample Circle Formats*, provides examples of Circles we have held with women in a corrections facility. It is called "sample" formats because, although you may choose to follow what we have done exactly, these formats are intended to serve simply as starting points—suggestions for how a Circle devoted to exploring values might be designed for your participants.

The purpose of this book is to explain how metaphors can enrich our lives and lead to deeper dialogues about our values. Read the book straight through, or skip around to the sections that interest you. This book is designed as a guide; please use it in whatever way is most effective for you.

PART 1

Using Metaphors to Explore Values in Circles

Exploring the
Values We Live By

Values are our compass in life. The values we
bring to a situation determine how we respond.
Before dealing with any conflict, therefore, we
need to clarify our values. What values can help
us work through our differences in the best way
possible?

Exploring people's experiences around
values plays a vital role in bringing a Circle
together. . . . Such questions as "What is real
courage?" or "What do honesty and trust require?" have no pat answers, yet how we understand these values affects how we act on them.

Though we may not be able to practice all our
values fully, we nonetheless need them to guide
us. We continually clarify our values not to
admonish ourselves for failing to act on them
adequately, but to help us make choices that
reflect how we most want to be.

· Kay Pranis, Barry Stuart, and Mark Wedge,
Peacemaking Circles

Values form the core of human life. They shape who we are, what
we do, and how we do it. When differences arise, values guide

our responses. Values inform how we raise our children, and they mold us into the kind of people we become. They set their stamp on the quality of our relationships, and they mold the character of our families, communities, and nations. Our values are there to support us in our best and our most painful times. Indeed, values are a matter of our survival.

In *The Lakota Way: Stories and Lessons for Living*, Joseph M. Marshall III shares stories from his own Sicangu Lakota tradition that teach about virtues (which we discuss here as values)—e.g., humility, compassion, love, bravery, respect, and generosity—and how these virtues translate into everyday life. Introducing these stories, he writes about the role that these virtues have played in the survival of his nation:

> The virtues espoused by the stories in this book were and are the foundation and moral sustenance of Lakota culture. There is nothing more important. It isn't that we don't care about physical comfort or material possessions, it is because we don't measure ourselves or others by those things. We believe we are measured by how well, or how little, we manifest virtues in our life's journey.
>
> When life for us was forever altered by the arrival of Europeans—when entire populations were devastated by disease, alcohol, war, and dispossession—we survived by living by the virtues we learned from our stories. We relied on being the kind of people our stories told us our ancestors had been, and thereby we remained true to ourselves and to them, and we are still surviving. [(New York: Penguin Compass, 2001), xiii]

We don't conclude from his words that some people or groups have values and others don't; our assumption is that we all have values. For better or worse, values are embedded in our ways of being. The issue is *which* values we choose to rely on in shaping our lives, families, communities, and nations. Or in Marshall's terms, which values are also virtues? Which values help us become the kind of people we most want to be?

To begin this exploration into our values, we might pose such questions as

+ Which values are important to us?
+ How did these particular values come to be important?
+ What have our experiences been around these values?
+ How are the actual values we live by—which may or may not be the same as those we regard as good or virtuous—expressed in our lives, relationships, communities, and nation?

Because values affect every aspect of who we are, exploring our values is a process that directly impacts us. Talking about our values renews us. It also purifies and humbles us, as we may discover that the values we have been bringing to our relationships are not those we really wanted to bring. One way or another, exploring our values resets our compass and gives us greater access to our deepest sources of energy, vision, and hope. Working with values becomes a force for personal as well as collective change. It helps us remember our sense of meaning within "the big picture," whether as individuals, families, communities, or as a nation. Indeed, touching base with our values gives us the depth of moral support that we often need to keep going. The experience is inevitably transforming, all the more so when we engage in the process together.

Circles as Places to Give Voice to Our Values

Circles create an ideal space where we can explore our values together. Historically and traditionally, Indigenous cultures worldwide have used various Circle processes to express and reinforce their values, and these value-centered dialogues have played vital roles in maintaining community harmony.

In contrast to these traditions, the dominant Euro-American society does not generally provide forums for exploring common values in ways that are integrated with our social, political, educational, and family experiences. Mindfulness of our values—which values matter to us and how we go about living them—is not something that most of us living in the dominant society have many opportunities to consider deeply or critically together. Yet drifting out of touch with our values is dangerous. If we read history books written from the point of view of the oppressed, such as Howard Zinn's *A People's History of the United States* (1980, 2003) and James Loewen's *Lies My Teacher Told Me* (1995), or consider the facts of global warming, we are reminded just how devastating the consequences can be of losing sight of our best values—not just in personal lives but also in history and in the natural and human worlds.

To address this cultural gap, we seek in this book to help Circle keepers create a space where participants can give voice to their values. We have witnessed time and again the unifying effect of this shared exploration. Circles promote a sense of safety that encourages participants to talk about their life journeys. As participants open up about their experiences with values, they begin to see common ground, even among diverse groups struggling with painful and divisive issues. The deeper sharing reinforces individual dignity while honoring the unique quality of each person's thoughts and feelings. An environment is created that is so imbued with respect that participants find themselves able to say "yes" to the transformative power inherent in the process.

As sacred spaces, Circles allow our minds and spirits to work together for self-healing and for resolving whatever difficult issues we may face in transformative ways. When Circles focus not on this or that problem—even in Circles created to deal with a specific problem—but on values and the creative expression of them, they cause us to shift our thinking and problem-solving from our heads to our hearts. With this movement, we embark on a different way of addressing issues. The process unlocks

> "The Circle experience touched my spirit in many ways. It brought my spirit out."
>
> *–Circle participant incarcerated at the VOARCC*

our creativity and helps us move beyond the limitations imposed by existing emotional habits or linear thought. Inner shifts occur naturally. As our inner doors open, our hearts and spirits are freed to engage in problem-solving in ways that may not have otherwise occurred to us or that may have seemed impossible. In a real sense, the "prisoner" is released.

The Power of Value-Based Dialogue

This liberating effect of value-based dialogue lies at the core of Paolo Freire's classic work, *Pedagogy of the Oppressed*. For decades, Freire's book has been transforming not only education but also many people's approach to social change. Dialogue holds the power to overcome oppression, because, as he wrote, true dialogue contains no room for domination. If authentically engaged, its ultimate goal—and inevitable effect—is to transform both the victim and the perpetrator, the oppressed and the oppressor.

But not all dialogue can do this. The kind of dialogue that has a liberating, transformative effect must be based on specific values. For example, the values that go with ranking human beings in hierarchies of one-sided supremacy, privilege, and top-down control inspire not dialogue but simply more coercion and oppression.

The specific values that Freire names as essential to dialogue—without which true dialogue cannot occur—are love, humility, bravery, patience, courage, the search for truth, faith in human-kind, mutual trust, hope, and, last but certainly not least, critical thinking. Without a sincere commitment to practicing these values and bringing them to our dialogues, dialogue quickly de-generates into various forms of domination—a point he makes throughout the book. About the values essential to dialogue, Freire writes:

> Dialogue cannot exist . . . in the absence of a profound love for the world and for people. The naming of the world, which is an act of creation and re-creation, is not possible if it is not infused with love. Love is at the same time the foundation of dialogue and dialogue itself. . . .
>
> Because love is an act of courage, not of fear, love is commitment to others. . . . As an act of bravery, love can-not be sentimental; as an act of freedom, it must not serve as a pretext for manipulation. It must generate other acts of freedom; otherwise it is not love. . . . If I do not love the world—if I do not love life—if I do not love people—I cannot enter into dialogue.
>
> On the other hand, dialogue cannot exist without humility. The naming of that world, through which people constantly re-create that world, cannot be an act of arrogance. . . . How can I dialogue if I regard myself as a case apart from others—mere "its" in whom I cannot recognize other "I's"? How can I dialogue if I consider myself a member of the in-group of "pure" men, the own-ers of truth and knowledge, for whom all non-members are "these people" or "the great unwashed"? . . .
>
> Dialogue further requires an intense faith in human-kind, faith in their power to make and remake, to create and re-create, faith in their vocation to be more fully

human (which is not the privilege of an elite, but the birthright of all). . . .

Founding itself upon love, humility, and faith, dialogue becomes a horizontal relationship of which mutual trust between the dialoguers is the logical consequence. . . .

Nor yet can dialogue exist without hope. Hope is rooted in men's incompletion, from which they move out in constant search—a search which can be carried out only in communion with others. . . . The dehumanization resulting from an unjust order is not a cause for despair but for hope, leading to the incessant pursuit of the humanity denied by injustice. . . .

Finally, true dialogue cannot exist unless the dialoguers engage in critical thinking—thinking which discerns an indivisible solidarity between the world and the people and admits of no dichotomy between them—thinking which perceives reality as process, as transformation, rather than as a static entity. . . . For the critic, the important thing is the continuing transformation of reality . . . [(New York: Continuum, 1970, 30th Anniversary Edition, 2001), 89–92.]

Circles are places where participants put into practice what Freire describes. As we use Circles to explore our values, we enhance our personal capacity to live from our values in a conscious way. But the benefit of these Circles does not stop with personal change. We also learn how to engage in dialogue that is truly liberating from all kinds of oppression—internal and external, within our personal relationships as well as within our societies and between peoples. We experience what it feels like to engage with others in non-dominating ways, to hold each other accountable as equal contributors in a process of change, and to work for a sense of good and justice that is genuinely inclusive. The more we connect with our values through dialogue, the more the dialogue itself becomes value-based, and the more powerful it becomes as a force for transformation. In Freire's terms, through value-based dialogues, we take part in the practice of liberation.

The Power of Metaphors

Metaphors are all around us; it is only a matter of noticing them.

How can we begin exploring our values? It's not always easy. Values can seem abstract and unrelated to the nitty-gritty of everyday life, especially to those sitting in prison or a classroom. As we explain later on, our Circles with the women who were incarcerated didn't take off until we started using metaphors to facilitate the dialogue. Looking back, we realize that using metaphors to discuss values is entirely natural and obvious. People the world over use metaphors to ponder life's intangibles and have done so for millennia. When asked about values, seldom do people talk in theories or abstractions. Instead, they launch into a story or invoke some familiar image.

Metaphors are powerful for good reason. They help us tap into powers that we all have for healing and transformation that surpass our trained intellects. When we are in conflict or pain, the best logic does very little to help. Deep, transformative shifts are far more likely to occur when someone shares a personal story or appeals to an image. If the metaphor fits, it takes hold of us, gives us a different perspective, and moves us to an inner place where change becomes possible.

How Metaphors Work

Metaphors work by juxtaposing two dissimilar things in order to get us to think about each more creatively. When Shakespeare wrote "All the world's a stage," for instance, he was using the metaphor of a stage to invite us to think differently about the world. The metaphors we use in this book juxtapose tangible, physical things with intangible, nonphysical values. The juxtaposition triggers our curiosity and unlocks our imagination. Before we know it, wondrous and unexpected insights emerge. Values come alive in ways we never thought about before. We make the leap from our everyday, habituated ways of thinking to freer, more spiritual perspectives—perspectives that take in wider possibilities. Metaphors help us think in ways that are not habitual for most of us but are, in fact, highly creative—"out of the box."

The power of metaphors comes from their use of concrete images. These images make us shift from our left-brained, analyze-and-calculate minds to our right brain—our holistic, intuitive, relation-oriented, and fundamentally creative minds. We process meaning through our right brain's powers, because our right brains think in wholes and relationships. Whereas our left brains excel at taking things apart in order to make critical analyses, our right brains excel at taking a holistic view and seeing how everything hangs together with meaning and purpose.

Given these powers, our right brains are the masters of our transformative, rebalancing potentials. Through our right-brain abilities, we experience ourselves as whole. That is why we are so distressed and act so crazily, even self-destructively, when our innate sense of wholeness feels violated. Our right brains set the mandate for wholeness and accept no less. If we are experiencing ourselves as whole, we are happy. If not, we are miserable and prone to act destructively, not to destroy ourselves but to call our own attention to our need to regain our wholeness.

Maintaining our wholeness as we change and go through life is our right brain's job. To do this work, our right brains need support. Whereas our left brains feed on data and critical analyses, our right brains thrive on metaphors and images. They are, in a sense, meaning junkies. They are stimulated not by new facts, which tend to reinforce existing views, but with new perspectives, which recast everything in a broader, more holistic, more meaningful framework.

In another classic book, *Man's Search for Meaning*, Viktor Frankl, a Jewish psychologist who survived several years in multiple Nazi concentration camps, concluded that we human beings can endure almost any "what" if we can find some sense of "why"—a sense of meaning to our lives. More than food or physical necessities, meaning sustains us. For these reasons, the powers we need for engaging in the kind of dialogue that is healing, transforming, and liberating are far more effectively accessed through metaphors than through intellectualizing or abstract thinking, important as these abilities are for other purposes.

The Connection between Metaphors and Values

We have come to believe that discussing values is essential to setting the focus, pace, and safety of a Circle. It can, in fact, be critical to a Circle's effectiveness. This is especially true in a diverse, multicultural environment—such as a corrections center—where inappropriate assumptions and misunderstandings inevitably occur. Discussing our values can transform a negative, alienating experience into something positive, because it can serve as a bridge, reconnecting us after rifts.

Yet exploring common values usually requires an intentional conversation. We must mutually decide to do it—voluntarily and by free will—and then we have to decide how. This is where metaphors come in. Besides making values seem less abstract, metaphors also give us a degree of separation from the immediate problem. Framed by a good metaphor, the images in our minds are no longer exclusively of a painful situation or conflict but also of the metaphor, which provides a different perspective.

As a result, using metaphors makes Circle dialogues less academic, institutional, or linear and much more creative. Rather than talking directly about a crime that was committed, for example, participants can use metaphors to represent situations—as well as their feelings about those situations—in non-threatening, non-judgmental, and non-accusatory ways. A good metaphor leaves the door open for hope. The adversarial format that usually accompanies efforts to deal with harms is replaced by an inclusive format—one that invites people to draw upon the healing values inherent in reparation and resolution. Circle participants are more likely to feel that they are "all on the same side" in their search for truth, justice, and good. The natural result is that value-focused Circles help unify rather than further separate already divided relationships.

> "No matter how I feel, when entering the Circle space, I feel a sense of a beautiful spirit or a presence around me. I trust the way I feel when I am in the Circle. The Circle experience is a support to me and to my family."
>
> *–Circle participant incarcerated at the VOARCC*

Sharing personal experiences around values plays a critical role in helping participants do this. As participants use the metaphors to reflect on their experiences, they recognize what they have in common and feel less divided, less isolated. Participants relax and allow the spirit to manifest through them. In a natural way, metaphors move people into a realm of spiritual sensitivity. Circle participants feel connected to others, and the connection feels good and nurturing, rather than threatening or abusive, as many of their personal relationships may have felt in the past. Slowly, participants see possibilities for becoming whole and changing their lives. Here again, exploring values through metaphors can support participants as they make changes, since transforming one's entire way of life is a challenging and often overwhelming process.

THE POWER OF METAPHORS   15

Choosing Appropriate Metaphors

Where do we find good metaphors, and how do we select the best ones to use for a particular value or situation? Metaphors are all around us. The trick lies in noticing them. As we take notice of simple images in our daily lives and then start working with these images as metaphors, the metaphors begin to "wake us up" from our habitual ways of seeing things. A situation may not have changed, but we view it differently, and this inner shift opens new options for how we might respond.

In choosing which metaphors to use in a Circle, we have sought to stay focused on the issues that the participants face and to select metaphors that speak directly to them. If, for example, the Circle's intent was to resolve a conflict, we looked for metaphors that might trigger a deeper understanding of the sources and energies fueling the conflict. If healing was the Circle's focus, we looked for metaphors that would suggest how to move through pain to physical, mental, emotional, relational, or spiritual healing. If the Circle's goal was to support participants through a rough period, we looked for metaphors that conveyed a sense of comfort, support, and reassurance.

In one of our Circles, for example, the participants chose the metaphor of a rope with many knots in it to symbolize the challenges that the woman faced in her healing process. The rope represented the woman's life, and each knot in the rope symbolized the issues and circumstances that not only led up to her commission of a crime but also kept her entangled with this event. Those participating in the Circle—her family, friends, and members of her community—spent over a year releasing the knots one by one as the woman faced her fears and met her responsibilities. Through the process, the woman was gradually able to work creatively with the other Circle participants in making reparations and transforming her life.

When the last knot was finally untied, the Circle closed with the woman holding on to the straightened rope—a graphic reminder of the year she had spent unraveling a complex array of painful experiences. In a later Circle, we presented the woman with a photo of the Circle members and participants framed by the untangled rope. The rope then symbolized the effort, trust, and understanding that had developed over the course of the year. With the Circle's support, she had worked long and hard to smooth out all the obstacles that had prevented her from expressing herself fully and in a good way.

In another Circle focused on the value of forgiveness, we opened by talking about two rocks we had brought to the session. Holding a rock in each hand, we talked about the individual properties of the rocks, and then we asked: "What do these two rocks have in common?" Before passing the talking piece that indicates which participant has the floor, we passed the two rocks around the Circle in opposite directions, inviting the participants to consider what the rocks had in common. It was a difficult question for them to answer; that is, until both rocks finally came into the hands of one person. After some reflection, the person realized that the two rocks fit together perfectly and had actually been one rock that had broken in two. The rocks, once whole, were literally reunited through the careful handling and observation of the Circle participants. With this metaphor fresh in mind, we passed the talking piece around the Circle and invited participants to speak about any personal relationships that had been broken and that now needed thought, observation, compassion, and careful handling in order to be mended.

In a Circle with teenage boys, we arranged for a huge refrigerator box to be delivered in a pickup truck to the parking lot where the Circle was being held. Then we had the coordinators send all the boys outside to bring the box into the building and carry it up to the room. The boys had to negotiate getting the box through all sorts of doors and narrow spaces. They faced challenges and had to work through them together. Finally, we had them set the box in the middle of the circle of chairs. The box was so big that they could not see the person who was sitting across from them.

During the Circle, we talked about what sits between us that is so big that we cannot "see" each other. We talked about how they worked together to carry the box up to the room. Why did they give so much energy to this task? What was so important to them about the box? What was their motivation in helping perfect strangers bring up such a big box? What motivated them to do things in their daily lives? Were they ready to help others when asked? What "big things" did they want to give their energy to and work on in order to make a difference in their lives and world? And so on. Without the tangible metaphor of the box and the physical experience of interacting with it, the boys most likely would have had a difficult time opening up to us and sharing what they were feeling.

At the VOARCC, we used the metaphor of a locked door. We arrived early, so that, when the women were brought down to the room, the door was locked. (We had shared with the staff what we were going to do.) The women asked the staff to open the door, and she told them that they would have to knock on the door. When they knocked, we told them that they would have to figure out how to get in, if that was what they truly wanted. A conversation through the door ensued, as we asked such questions as: Why do you want to open this door? What do you expect to find inside? What do you need to do in order to get these doors open? Finally, the women turned to the staff and begged her to use the key. She agreed, given that they seemed fairly determined to go inside. She added that the level of energy and interest that they had expressed could serve them well with any locked door they might face in their lives. When she opened the door, the women entered with some frustration. However, we had prepared the room with a lit candle and soft music playing to create a soothing atmosphere. During the Circle, we explored the metaphor of the locked door: Which locked doors did they wish to open in their lives, and which steps might they need to take once the doors were opened?

In another situation, a judge recommended a Circle for city personnel and neighbors to address neighborhood disputes that involved racism. We recommended to the keeper of the Circle that the chairs be placed in a circle with each chair facing away from the center. We wanted to have a few passes with the participants turned away from each other. This would give everyone an experience of having things said behind their backs. We also wanted to show participants how hard it is to develop good communication or relations when we don't "face" the people with whom we really need to be talking. Unfortunately, the facilitators of the initial Circle did not accept this suggestion. Nonetheless, such a metaphor could have enhanced the sharing and given voice to the strong feelings in the community that were being ignited around the destructive undercurrents of racism.

We share these examples to illustrate our premise that metaphors are everywhere. The trick lies in noticing them and then in using them to generate Circle dialogues. When the right metaphor for the right value comes together with the right group of participants, Circle dialogues go places that no one could have planned beforehand. Transformation that otherwise seemed unthinkable not only happens but even seems natural.

storytelling

Sharing a story releases personal truths. Once freed, our truths can be reclaimed. Reclaiming our truths, we feel their power, and healing begins.

Using metaphors and sharing stories from our lives go hand in hand. Metaphors unlock values by inspiring us to think about our experiences in different ways. The point is neither the metaphors nor the values per se but how they help us connect with who we are, and we do this by reflecting on our experiences. The real work begins, then, when we start telling our stories.

When we share our stories, we learn from each other, but more than that, we come to know and accept ourselves better. The time we spend listening to each other respectfully, compassionately, and nonjudgmentally teaches us to listen to ourselves with the same acceptance. Not only *what* we share but also *how* we share changes us.

We all have stories, and each of these stories contains elements of our authenticity and truth. Some of us have opportunities to tell our stories, while others do not. Much of our behavior seems influenced by the degree to which we feel our stories have been heard. In turn, our sense of being heard is influenced by the degree to which we have been able to give voice to our stories in trustworthy, safe environments. We believe that when our personal stories are heard and respected, the process of healing and empowerment begins. This belief drew us to become Circle keepers, and it has been continually reinforced by our experiences with the residents at the VOARCC.

Storytelling is a gift we make both to ourselves and to our communities. It helps us move away from the lonely, isolated spaces created by our internal voices on one hand and the social roles that separate us on the other. In the words of a Native elder, "The longest journey you'll ever make is from head to heart." As we make this journey, we find our personal truth—our heart's truth—and within that truth sits the teller of our stories.

> "What I like most about the Circle is its sacredness. I have the chance to release a piece of myself by sharing my story and reaching a spiritual place inside myself. I used to stuff my feelings down deep inside. The talking Circle taught me to open myself up."
>
> —Circle participant incarcerated at the VOARCC

Telling our stories from the heart brings unexpected inner resolutions not just in the storytellers but in the listeners as well. By reminding us of our strengths and commonalities, our hearts' stories give us confidence that we can, in fact, transform our personal and shared realities.

Yet we need safe, receptive spaces for this depth of sharing to occur. How many of us have felt a need to talk about an experience in a deep way but held back because in the past we have been silenced, no one was there to listen, or our story was dismissed as unimportant? Circles that hold values at the center provide the space we need to speak from our hearts and to know that we will be heard in a good way. The values remind participants to bring their best selves to the dialogue, while the Circle process establishes healthy boundaries for the exchange. Together, the values and the Circle process create an atmosphere where we can release our stories with clarity and then trust that they will be received with compassion. The more we share, the more we are able to share, and transformation occurs not for one person alone but for everyone involved. Ultimately, understanding how to develop a safe space—perhaps the most essential feature of the Circle process—is what makes this depth of sharing possible.

But where can these Circles be held? The better question is, where can't they be held? Circles can create healing, transformative, liberating spaces almost anywhere.

Planting Seeds of Change in People and Systems

I am so moved by the openness of the women in the Circle. Even in jail we can remain sisters and love and support each other.

· *Circle participant incarcerated at the VOARCC*

Developing our values is a life's journey, and rightly so, since values speak to what is most meaningful in our lives. They form the basic texture of cultures—what shapes our belief systems, religious views, economic systems, educational and health-related systems, and political institutions, including the criminal justice system. All of these systems are built on values and, in turn, these systems powerfully influence which values prevail. Society's systems and institutions actively promote and perpetuate the values on which they are based.

The Criminal Justice System and Values

The criminal justice system, for example, operates on values of rewards and punishments, which create hierarchies of who deserves what. Accordingly, many of those caught in the criminal justice system feel that they are bad people, deserving only of punishment, and that society judges them to be unworthy of compassion, understanding, or forgiveness. The fact that many if not most of those in prison feel consumed by values associated with intense self-rejection is no surprise, since these are precisely the values that shape every facet of the criminal justice system. It consistently reinforces the negative self-image, low self-esteem, and lack of self-worth that many inmates suffer, and this hurtful treatment heightens resentments, frustrations, anger, and despair. Yet these are precisely the kind of negative values that lead some people to commit crimes in the first place. At immense costs in human suffering and taxpayer dollars, the values of the current system set up a vicious cycle that in many cases reinforces, extends, and escalates harm. No wonder the recidivism rate is so high.

How might we change the criminal justice system so that it would help those who are incarcerated to embrace positive values—values that encourage self-respect and respect for others? More fundamentally, how might we rethink our ways of responding to harms? These are critical questions, since changing our paradigm of how we "do justice" could arguably reduce and even ultimately eliminate recidivism.

Contemplating such a shift begins with a long look at our values. We might ask:

- ◆ Which values do we bring to resolving conflicts and responding to harms?
- ◆ Is punishment (as a value) capable of creating the sense of self-worth and well-being, the capacities to be contributing members of society, and the good relationships that those in trouble clearly need in order to avoid future problems?
- ◆ If we believe that compassion, understanding, and forgiveness are values that support the good in human beings, where in the criminal justice system can those who are incarcerated learn, witness, and experience these values and thus have their lives improved by them?

As the criminal justice system now operates, experiences of positive human values are intentionally denied to prisoners. We heard residents comment, "I am not treated like a human being here"; "I am looked down on." They talked about how the system does not demonstrate respect for those incarcerated, for their relationships, or for their families, especially their children. During visits with their children and other family members, for example, physical exchanges of affection and care were routinely forbidden. Yet all human beings need affection, and children especially need it from their mothers, regardless of their mothers' circumstances. How can both the women's and children's needs and the system's concerns for safety be better met?

Based on our work with those incarcerated, we have observed that the criminal justice system is almost entirely vested in focusing on the crime and in regarding the perpetrator of the crime as nothing more than a criminal—the epitome of "the degraded Other." It refuses to see that those living inside prisons are human beings who have apparently made bad choices and who need support in rectifying those harms and constructing new lives. Instead of taking this positive approach, the system operates from the dominant value of returning harm for harm by maximizing humiliation, emotional pain, isolation, and hardship. Its only purpose is to degrade and to cause suffering—to punish.

Applying a New Set of Values

Value-focused Circles are in every way antithetical to the criminal justice system. It was never our idea that introducing Circles could somehow improve or change the criminal justice system— not as long as punishment dominates as the organizing value. However, we could offer an alternative experience in the midst of this hurtful environment to those women who were open to it and who volunteered to participate.

Value-centered Circles introduced to this alienating system a totally different response to what had happened in the women's lives. Metaphorically speaking, the Circles created a space for the seed of basic human respect to crack through the concrete of systematic degradation and dehumanization, so that new ways of being could blossom. When the residents worked with the Circle process during their incarceration, they saw how applying a new set of values in their relationships could radically change their lives and experiences. Above all, they felt what it was like to be treated respectfully and to treat others respectfully in return. The Circles gave participants time to reflect on life-affirming values and to develop tools for integrating these values into their lives when they left the corrections center.

During the Circles, we listened to how the participants understood each value and what their experiences around that value had been. The women's beliefs and opinions varied widely and their diverse views reflected a multitude of backgrounds, cultures, educational opportunities, and life experiences. Although many of the women acknowledged that values were important to them, they didn't know how to integrate positive, life-affirming values into their own lives.

> "I can't express what the talking Circle does to make me feel safe in this place. The Circle takes me away from here for a short time. It has a way of making me feel worthwhile and loved."
>
> –Circle participant incarcerated at the VOARCC

When they first started to think about values, most of the women drew on experiences from their early childhoods. For example, some recognized the importance of honesty, yet in their early lives, neither their parents nor their caretakers had exhibited much honesty. In their middle and later childhood years, values were not talked about much, if at all. For most of the women, life was about survival and was driven by a largely negative set of values. One woman, for example, spoke of greed as the ruling value in her life. She came from poverty and disadvantage, and she was taught that she had a right to steal and manipulate. It was acceptable for her to take from others in order to give herself a chance and perhaps make her own life better.

As Circle keepers, we were responsible for helping to maintain the sacred space for such personal revelations, but to do this, we had to fully absorb what the women were saying, and this took time. The women also needed time to absorb what they were experiencing in the Circles. They learned that bringing positive values to the surface of their lives was indeed possible, and they displayed incredible courage in their work to do this. In spite of everyday dehumanization, the women began to feel worthy of experiencing nurturing values in ways that had been systematically denied them.

> "What an honor to watch the changes a person can make because of community involvement—experiencing, maybe for the first time, the values of honesty, respect, spirituality, humility, and compassion."
>
> –Kay Longtin, Cottage Grove, Minnesota, peacemaking Circle participant

One woman, for example, stated that the Circle had been the best and most practical experience she had had in prison, because, again, it had given her an opportunity to relate to others with respect and to be treated with respect. It helped her understand the other women in the Circle, and it allowed her to practice patience and tolerance with those whom she disliked or with whom she disagreed. Another woman found that holding Circles with her children after her release gave her kids time to be heard, to talk about their feelings, and to be more considerate of other family members. She said her children really understood the Circle process and thrived within it.

Taking the Circle process into prisons is not for everyone, of course. And holding Circles in any institution—whether it be a youth center, school, church, nonprofit organization, social service unit, shelter, community justice program, professional office, business, corporation, or boardroom—can be overwhelming and downright discouraging at times. At those moments, we remind each other that our expectations are not the appropriate measuring sticks for "success" and that things may need to be worked out that we know nothing about. We remind each other to trust the Circle process and to trust the values.

Sometimes we do not learn about the full effect of a Circle until years later when we run into someone at the grocery store or post office and discover how her life has been transformed by her experiences in Circle. After many years, we have come to view our Circle work as planting seeds of change in both people and institutions—not only the most oppressed people but also the most oppressive institutions. As with the growth of seeds, the process takes time. Long periods can pass when it looks as if nothing is happening. Yet just when we find ourselves struggling with doubts or discouragement is often when we realize that our next Circle happens to be about patience or trust or humility or love. So we keep going.

> "I would like to see the process used broadly, so that others can experience the inner peace that comes with the free and protected exchange of feelings and thoughts."
>
> *–Circle participant incarcerated at the VOARCC*

How Our Journey with Circles Developed

Circles often begin with inviting people to introduce themselves and to describe how they came to be a part of that particular Circle. This practice "locates" people and emphasizes the journey-like nature of our lives. Certain steps brought us to where we are, and sharing our journeys creates a context in which we can begin to understand and appreciate each other. In this spirit, we would like to share the personal journeys that have brought us to our work with Circles, values, and metaphors, and hence to writing this book.

Sue's Story

When my youngest daughter was three years old, she attended the Salvation Army Preschool in our neighborhood. As we were leaving school one day, I noticed an attractive poster announcing that the Women of Nations Eagle's Nest Shelter was holding a feast of gratitude and appreciation; everyone was invited. I was moved to attend with my daughter. It was autumn and cool, so it felt good to be inside. We followed our noses to where the feast was being held and were welcomed by the women hosting the event. To my surprise, one of the women looked at my little girl and invited me to take her to one side of the room to receive some gifts. In disbelief at their generosity, we walked across the room where men were singing as they beat a drum. After receiving our gifts, we were directed to sit at a table. Joining others who were already seated there, we introduced ourselves to each other. A woman in the front of the room then introduced the Eagle's Nest Women's Shelter and expressed gratitude and appreciation to everyone there. I thought, "These folks are walking their talk."

Some people who would become very special in my life were present at that feast. Sitting at my table was Pat Thalhuber, and on that day eleven years ago, we began our journey together. Believing that we are not meant to always be in control but to touch and be touched by those we meet, Pat and I discussed our mutual belief in the value of the personal stories that we each carry and their potential importance for others as well. By sharing our stories right there at the feast, we realized that we had a common desire and need to express ourselves through storytelling. Together, Pat and I have pursued these convictions with others through our participation in talking Circles.

In 1998, Pat invited me to join her in creating a place for talking Circles at a women's prison, the VOARCC. Initially, Circle attendance was small, and on one occasion, no one came at all. When women did attend, they were distracted. Almost immediately, we realized that in order to create a meaningful space that would nurture safety and openness for the women, we needed to introduce a Circle component that would be supportive, that would lend direction to the dialogue, and that would draw the women out.

I remember the first time I set foot in the VOARCC. I had never been in a women's prison before. I was anxious and alert. The small room we were given for the Circle was filled with eight women—women I had never met before and probably would never have met had I not been there for the Circle. I honored that realization, feeling both respect and gratitude. Once again I was reminded that those who cross my path hold a piece of my life's puzzle—that this is the mystery of life. The women found a place to sit and waited for us to begin. As I observed the women who chose to come, I noticed that some held a slouched posture—a deliberate slouch.

We began by explaining the talking Circle process. By the time of this Circle, we were already using the pilot Circle program we had developed called "Building a Home for the Heart." After introducing the participants to the Circle process, we began the Circle by engaging the metaphor of a home and correlating the different rooms in the home to particular values. As we explained the metaphor, some of the participants were obviously inattentive, and they made it clear that they considered it a chore to be there. Yet as the talking piece moved slowly around the Circle and each woman had an opportunity to share her thoughts without being interrupted, we noticed a distinct shift in the participants' attention. Their postures changed, and they became more present. Gradually and almost in spite of themselves, they were choosing to be with us.

Once we saw how using the house metaphor had helped the women open up, we realized that we needed to talk about values in different ways in order to create a consistently safe place for them. We asked the women to think about the values that were important to them, and we have incorporated those values into our Circles with this group of women. We have also continued to invite the women to share their views on how to maintain a safe place in the Circle.

From that beginning, Circle attendance grew. Building trust with the women involved a long journey; it did not happen overnight. As time passed, though, we realized that it was our use of metaphors that was helping the women connect with their values and their experiences around them—positive and negative—in ways they had never done before. The metaphors functioned like keys unlocking a deeper wisdom in the women. Simple and basic as the metaphors were, they enabled us to create together a safe environment where the women could let down their defenses, open their hearts, and share their stories.

Pat's Story

It is time to embrace the demons.
It is time to release the prisoner.
It is time to master the fear.

It is time to surrender control.
It is time to transform the negative.
It is time to manifest change.

It is time to welcome possibility.
It is time to nourish the positive.
It is time to say, "Yes."

It is time to be grateful.
    It is time.
        It is time.
        It is time.

I read this poem of mine at the close of a talking Circle at the VOARCC in Roseville, Minnesota. In a simple way, the poem summarizes our journey of using metaphors in value-centered Circles as a way to support dialogue and social change.

My work with Sue began when we both attended a gathering to discuss domestic abuse. Over lunch, Sue and I talked about the fear, negativity, loss of control, and sense of imprisonment that women in these circumstances experience. During the next several months, our conversations continued, and, as a result of our discussions, Sue joined me in my work with Circles Restored, an outreach program in the Minneapolis–St. Paul, Minnesota, area.

Circles Restored used the Circle process to help families, especially homeless families, connect with community resources to resolve personal and family issues. By offering families a problem-solving process in which their experiences could be heard and respected, these Circles gave them the confidence to move forward and make changes. The agencies participating in the work of Circles Restored found the Circle process to be effective, productive, and rewarding.

Following the close of Circles Restored, Sue and I continued our work together by participating in the Circle trainings offered by the Dakota County Corrections. During that time, a few of us initiated Circle processes at the juvenile justice center in Hastings, Minnesota, as well as at other facilities in the Twin Cities area. Sue and I then began to introduce talking Circles at the VOARCC.

Based on our success in using values and metaphors in talking Circles over many years, we feel moved to pass on our experiences to you as professionals, communities, families, teachers, students, activists, and individuals. We hope that you will consider integrating values and metaphors into your Circle processes and will come to experience the healing that can occur within the sacred space of your own Circles.

The Story of Our Circles as the VOARCC

There are some things I need to tell you;
Some things you need to hear.
Be honest, please be true;
Let me level with you, Dear.

I've told you many lies;
I've even stolen your money.
I've taken kindness for weakness.
I'm so sorry, Honey.

I need to change my life—
Try going left instead of right.
I'm really scared to give it up.
Am I strong enough for this fight?

I've built these walls that surround me—
To protect me, to serve me, to save me from me.
I want to rise up out of hell.
I will do whatever it takes to leave my private jail.

· Circle participant incarcerated at the VOARCC

We listened to this Circle participant share her poem with eleven other women at the Volunteers of American Regional Corrections Center. For someone coping with the realities of incarceration, she expressed a remarkable courage to say these things so openly. True, she was saying them in front of empathetic listeners and in an atmosphere of physical and emotional safety; even so, these were painful truths for her to express to anyone, most of all to herself. Such an extraordinary happening illustrates the power of the Circle to bring out the best in those present. Circles have a power that changes lives.

This power stems from the nature of the Circle space. In Circles, participants are able to engage the creative, unpredictable side of human expression, because they draw strength from what is constant about Circles: the respect, the listening, the thoughtful pace, the safety. From this strength, they gain the courage to explore the free, open, and expansive possibilities for saying what is in their minds and hearts. This balance between what is constant and what is unpredictable makes Circles safe enough for participants to take risks in addressing some of the hardest and most painful issues they face.

Setting the Stage for Circles

In our talking Circles at the VOARCC, we set the stage for the Circle experience. We started with the physical space. We arranged the chairs in a circle to accommodate the Circle process. We designed a circular centerpiece made of four pie-shaped, colored pieces of cloth, which we always placed in the middle of the floor. The colors of the cloths symbolized the four seasons: yellow for spring, green for summer, brown for autumn, and white for winter. We wrote the values that the women had chosen to focus on during the Circles on paper plates, which we put around the edges of each piece of cloth. We then placed a clay candle sculpture of women sitting in a circle in the middle of the centerpiece. When the women entered, they sat in the circle of chairs around our centerpiece.

We usually opened the Circle with a story, poem, thought, reading, or prayer—something that would help participants shift their focus from the prison environment to the Circle space. Following the Circle's opening, we always had a first pass for the women to check in and share how they were doing. After the check-in round, we would pose questions or ideas that the participants could think about and respond to if they wished during a round. When we finished our opening comments, we would then pass the talking piece to the person on our left. The participant could respond to the questions at hand, share other information, hold the talking peace for a moment in silence, or simply pass. From that person, the talking piece would continue to be passed around the Circle in one direction, until each participant had had an opportunity to either share or pass.

While serving as the Circle's keepers (a role described in the next section), we also participated like everyone else, sharing our thoughts and feelings whenever the talking piece came to us. When one person was sharing, everyone else listened silently. Although it was difficult to refrain from "cross talk"—jumping in to offer opinions, suggestions, or comments—we all knew that it was critical to the success of the Circle to show our respect for each speaker and to listen without interrupting her. Since most Circles had three passes or more, each person had at least three opportunities to share her thoughts and feelings.

Whenever a participant would share her story during one of the passes, her openness would encourage others to reflect on their lives and to share their stories as well. Each person who holds the talking piece is honored for her story and her presence in the Circle. Sharing personal experiences—storytelling—within the sacred

> "I liked being listened to. . . . This was a peaceful, expansive experience."
>
> –Circle participant incarcerated at the VOARCC

Circle space facilitates a distinct quality of listening and responding. Instead of thinking about what they want to say in response, listeners know they have to remain silent, and so they listen with a depth that is not common in everyday interactions. They concentrate on what is being expressed, rather than being distracted by mentally planning a response. As a result, listeners empathize with the speaker; they are more likely to set aside opinions and judgments and instead imagine and perhaps even feel what it is like to be someone else. This deep listening creates a sense of community, and participants begin to bond with each other.

As the Circle's process transformed the participants' ways of experiencing themselves and each other, we found that fears, negative judgments, and misconceptions could be confronted in spiritual and practical ways. Possibilities for understanding, clarity, and healing emerged—person by person, story by story. A Native elder once referred to this process as "living from the inside out."

In the Circles, participants found opportunities to forgive themselves, to seek forgiveness from others, to visit their "demons," as they called their addictions, and to walk through their fears. The road was not easy, yet for some women, the Circle process and the transformation it initiated continued beyond the walls of the corrections center.

After their release, in fact, some of the women invited us to continue the Circle process with them. Through Circles, we journeyed with several of the women and their families as they worked to reconstruct their lives and to live with dignity, respect, and integrity. For some, like the woman who shared her poem on honesty, our "re-entry" Circle dialogues helped them realize that they needed to leave the Twin Cities altogether and start new lives elsewhere. For others, their re-entry period involved a time of reclaiming their identity and simply starting afresh in different communities in the area. For most, it meant learning how to mend the harms they had caused.

Examples of Metaphors We Used

Looking back, we find that some of the metaphors we used stay with us more than others. Certainly the metaphor of the knotted rope symbolizing the woman's life stands out, since we worked with that image for an entire year.

> "The talking Circle is a wonderful tool for living. I hope others use it as much as I did, and I plan to continue using Circles in my life once I'm released."
>
> –Circle participant incarcerated at the VOARCC

In another Circle, we focused on the value of friendship, and we used the metaphor of individually woven bracelets with interlocking beads. We spent this Circle talking about how life is like a weaving with separate experiences merging to form pivotal moments, much like the beads on the bracelet. During the Circle, we broke the bracelets in half, and the participants witnessed something beautiful being destroyed and falling apart. The participants then discussed what had caused their relationships and friendships to break apart, as the bracelets had broken. We then asked them if they thought these relationships could be mended, and if so, how might the mending occur?

Yet another Circle focused on the metaphor of a key, which inspired many questions. For example: What does the key open? Where does the key come from? If I find what it opens, is it something I can use or treasure? Do I need to use the key? These questions then linked to larger life questions, such as: What is it that will open me up? Do I want to open up? If so, whom do I want to open up to? And if I do open up, what will it get me? Ultimately, asking such questions led to the realization that we will never be able to explore the answers to any of them unless we are willing to look at our lives in new and transformative ways.

From Metaphors to the Dance of the Circle

Our experiences at the VOARCC showed us that placing values at the center of the Circle process and using metaphors to explore them invite participants to experience a new rhythm—a partnership with each other in community. The metaphors we used set the Circle's rhythm in motion, and the Circle's beat developed as we listened with compassion and understanding to each others' stories. Before we knew it, a dance of connected creativity began. At the VOARCC, we could plan which values to talk about and the metaphors we hoped might spark reflection, but we could not plan the dance that followed when the Circle process went into full swing.

Incarcerated women have had to overcome many hardships in their lives—abuse, violence, rejection, addiction, racism for women of color, class-ism, and poverty. Sitting in Circles with these women allowed us to witness their stories. We are grateful and honored to have been able to develop a process with them that created a safe place in which they could voice their truths. Our society offers few places where we can speak without interruption, be heard, and share from our hearts—all the more so for those whom society does not privilege. That the Circle creates such a place and that this place holds great healing, transformative power are ultimately what makes the process we share so important.

> "The talking Circle gives me an inner serenity and peace. I really enjoy the comfortable surrounding that embraces me while I am in Circle. In the Circle, I feel that I can say whatever is on my mind without getting negative feedback or cut-downs from anyone. When leaving Circle, I always feel as though a part of me is free, and I have grown."
> —Circle participant incarcerated at the VOARCC

Some Circle Basics

The way of Circles becomes a way of life.

As keepers of many value-centered Circles, we are consistently reminded that the way keepers and participants present themselves from the beginning of the gathering greatly affects how the Circle proceeds. From the Circle's opening, therefore, we seek to create and hold a welcoming space. We also include the participants in any decision-making aspects of the Circle, so that they can "buy into" the process and make it relevant to their experiences.

Like many others who participate in and conduct Circles, we find that the Circle process is immensely flexible, responsive to the variations in personal sharing that take place. However, some elements stay constant, namely, those that set up the basic Circle framework. In this guide, you can assume that the following aspects of the Circle process function in a consistent way.

The Keeper(s)

The keeper is the person who opens and closes the Circle, facilitates the Circle's rounds or passes, develops the questions that guide the Circle process, selects the talking piece, makes sure that Circle participants feel welcomed and comfortable, and supplies the materials used during the Circle. Circles often have two keepers who work together, which was a good practice at our VOARCC Circles.

During the Circle, keepers serve to facilitate the flow of dialogue. They neither control nor direct the dialogue; they "keep" it. For example, at the beginning of each pass, it is definitely help-ful for the Circle keeper(s) to summarize what was shared in the previous pass and then to present some opening thoughts for the next round. They often frame the round-opening thoughts as a set of questions that can guide the sharing, although they always encourage participants not to feel bound by what they suggest. Very often issues come up—things that have happened in the participants' lives or emotions that surface—that require them to alter their plans, making changes for the following pass.

> "Circles give everyone an equal voice and an opportunity to share from the heart and listen with the heart. When doing that, compassion, understanding, and forgiveness flow into our lives."
>
> *—Maggie Clements,*
> *Circle of Harmony*
> *Team*

Above all, though, keepers engage in the Circle process as equal and commit-ted participants. As with everyone else who chooses to participate in a Circle, they do not hold themselves apart from the Circle in a place of distance, detach-ment, superiority, authority, or privilege. Keepers do not have—nor should they be expected to have—"the answers" to any issue that arises, neither do they have preconceived ideas about what needs to be expressed. It is always the Circle as a whole—all the participants together—who engage in addressing whatever is before them. The wisdom and power of a Circle resides in every-one, including those who choose to remain silent, and the respon-sibility for the safety and meaningfulness of a Circle experience is shared equally among those involved.

The Talking Piece

The Circle itself and all its elements can, of course, serve as meta-phors for values, and the talking piece is a good example. As par-ticipants grow accustomed to using a talking piece, they come to associate it with the value of respect. Simply holding the talking piece puts participants in a respectful frame of mind.

The talking piece used in Circles indicates whose turn it is to speak. It can be a feather, a rock, a book, a cup, a crystal—any manageable item that could lend further meaning to the dialogue. Because the talking piece often serves as a focal point for reflection, it helps if the Circle keeper selects a talking piece that supports the theme for the Circle session.

Circle participants hold the talking piece while they are speaking, and when they are finished speaking, they pass it to the participant on their left. Whoever holds the talking piece shares from the heart. The Circle members listen respectfully to each speaker; there is no cross talk with the person holding the talking piece. If participants wish to comment on what others have said, they wait until the talking piece comes to them to do so. This measured dynamic creates a respectful, reflective atmosphere quite different from the customary banter and back-and-forthing of everyday conversations.

> "I believe that the Circle began changes in me. It showed me what I wouldn't have realized unless I had the security of sharing with a talking piece. The Circle helped me face my addiction and my fears."
>
> –Circle participant incarcerated at the VOARCC

The Centerpiece

Like the talking piece, the centerpiece provides a visual focal point for the Circle gathering. A centerpiece can symbolize many things, but balance and equality in particular are important values to reinforce for the Circle process. They remind us that, in the Circle, we come together as equals and meet in the middle, sometimes from opposite poles. We have often lit a candle as a sign that the Circle is about to begin, and we have also arranged in the center natural objects—flowers, leaves, stones, or feathers—that reflect the season. Some Circle keepers suggest that participants bring objects that are meaningful to them either to hold during the Circle or, if invited, to place in the center as well.

The Circle Opening

Circle participants arrive at Circles from lives and worlds that contrast sharply with the tone and feel of a Circle. This was especially true of the women at the VOARCC. Prisons and Circles are at opposite ends of the respect spectrum. For this reason, keepers put considerable thought into deciding how to open a Circle, especially since beginnings can be challenging. A good Circle opening—whether it is a reading, a comment, or a simple action like lighting a candle—reorients participants to the Circle. Ideally, a good Circle opening invites participants to think in ways that unite rather than divide, heal rather than harm, and instill love rather than hate.

Rounds or Passes

A round of the talking piece refers to one circuit of passing the talking piece to each person around the Circle, giving each participant an opportunity to speak. Most Circles have at least three passes, but there can be as many rounds or passes as the participants wish to have. As we mentioned, at the end of a round, the keeper will generally make some summarizing comments and then pose some questions before beginning the next pass. In the following guide, even though we do not always mention in the text that we summarized what had been said during the previous pass, we always do this. It is a good way to affirm the value of what participants have shared, and it helps to keep the Circle dialogue focused.

Sometimes participants would rather not speak. Again, Circle participants are not required to respond. If they prefer, they can just listen. When the talking piece comes to them, they may either immediately pass it on or hold it a few moments to introduce a time of silence. The choice is theirs.

In our descriptions of Circle passes that follow, if we have no special suggestions for the pass, we will simply list the questions that we used to frame the sharing.

Closing Comments and Closing Gifts

Circle closings are as important as Circle openings, since they reinforce the experience as well as remind participants of what has transpired during their time together. A closing gift is one effective way to end a Circle session. Often the closing gift will reflect the season, the metaphors, or the value(s) that were discussed during the Circle. A closing gift can be as simple as a gesture, a handshake, or a reading, or it can be something tangible like a small card of encouragement, a shell, a leaf, or a flower. The closing gift is optional and need not be elaborate, and any gifts exchanged must comply with the institutional or community guidelines where the Circle is held.

At the corrections facility, these small tokens—of no particular value in themselves—served to ground our experiences together. They reminded the women of what they had heard and experienced of themselves and each other during the Circle, and they provided a simple focus for the women to carry with them until the next Circle meeting. For those in deep personal struggle, these tokens have often had a big effect in helping participants stay focused on their values and carry the Circle experience with them into their lives. If the gifts were small enough, they could put them in their pockets as a reminder when they

> "I believe in this process. It changed me. I learned a lot about forgiveness. Using the talking piece and being listened to without interruption allowed me to realize things about my relationships and about myself that may not have surfaced otherwise. It gave me the security to say what I felt. It helped me to be able to speak my desires, fears, and my anger."
>
> –Circle participant incarcerated at the VOARCC

were down or struggling. Whether keepers choose to include gifts or not, though, some closing words or gestures help to send participants off in a good way.

Confidentiality

Although Circle participants must work together to decide which values to bring to the dialogue, confidentiality is one value that must always be agreed upon before each Circle, because it guarantees privacy and safety for participants. Assuring confidentiality empowers participants to speak freely and openly. As keepers of the Circles held at the VOARCC, we took what was said in a Circle outside of that Circle only when it endangered an individual or the facility. When we took this action, we did so with the full knowledge and, when appropriate, consent of the participants. However, such situations rarely occurred. For the most part, what was spoken and heard during the Circle stayed within the Circle.

> "I would like to incorporate the values of the Circle in my life and relationships; I have seen the process work."
>
> –Circle participant incarcerated at the VOARCC

In sharing our experiences as keepers of value-oriented Circles in this book, we maintain our commitment to confidentiality, and we share stories, comments, poetry, and other specifics only when we have obtained permission from a Circle participant to do so.

Equality

Equality is another core value of the Circle process and is affirmed by it in many ways. For example, everyone sits at an equal distance to the center—a visual, spatial equality that is highlighted by a centerpiece. In the Circle space, titles are not generally used, and participants introduce themselves by their first names.

Participants then return to using the appropriate titles with each other when they interact outside the Circle. Many of those who have positions in law enforcement or the criminal justice system make a point to attend Circles in street clothes instead of their uniforms, again, to emphasize the equality among the Circle participants and to de-emphasize their roles in the hierarchies that exist outside the Circle.

During the Circle, each participant has an equal opportunity to speak, and the personal truths that participants express are equally respected. No one is better than others in the Circle—a feature of Circles that children and young people appreciate immediately. Again, the keepers do not stand above the Circle but participate like everyone else. Keepers serve as a place to begin and end the passes, but participants could always choose to change that if they wished.

In Circles, participants feel what it is like to be treated as equals in a space where equality is absolutely protected. This protected equal treatment contributes to the safety that participants feel, and it is most likely why many young people and those whose voices are not otherwise heard tend to blossom in Circles.

Circles as "Being Present" and as a Way of Life

As you see, Circles involve far more than putting chairs in a circle and talking. They also offer far more than a technique for facilitating discussions. Circles incorporate values into every element of the process, and to be in Circle is to come together in a deeply respectful, compassionate, and humble way. What matters most is not what we say—how persuasive, eloquent, or inspiring we can be. Giving a moving performance is not what counts. What matters most is how "present" we can be with each other. This presence is expressed in how we hold ourselves as we sit, how attentively and openly we listen, how we look at each other, how we smile and laugh, the extent to which we take what is said into our hearts and hold it with care, and, when we do speak, whether we speak respectfully and from our hearts. To be in Circle is to be in a sacred space, because the Circle invites each of us to bring the essence of who we are to the time we spend together.

No wonder, then, that spending time in Circle on a regular basis changes us. Being in Circle challenges many habits of modern life—the hurriedness, the impatience, the judgment, the urge to put down, the desire to impress, and the need to control. By being present with each other in a Circle way, we go to depths of self-awareness and compassion that few other places in our lives support. Going to these places—and in the ways that Circles take us there—is inevitably transforming. We leave Circles with a very different sense of ourselves and others, because we hold each other not with the usual opinions and judgments but with a sacredness that practicing Circle values inspires. Gradually, the way of Circles becomes a way of life.

Crafting Value-Based Circles

The Circle helped me stay focused on developing into the woman I am today. It brought things I knew to the surface, like being honest not only with myself but also with others. The Circle involved creativity: we were able to create things with markers to match the value of the Circle.

· *Circle participant incarcerated at the VOARCC*

In a discussion about values, it is not always easy for participants to talk about the deeper issues or to share what they feel. Yet sharing personal experiences with our values can be powerful and transformative. This is why we turned to metaphors.

In this guide, then, we offer suggestions for using the metaphors that seemed to be most helpful for the women in our Circle settings. We have found that the simpler the metaphors are, the more powerful they can become. For each of the twelve values we consider, we describe the main metaphor we used plus additional metaphors that have worked well in our VOARCC Circles. Each Circle format that we present in the following pages, therefore, includes

+ thoughts on the value's meaning to get the discussion going
+ ideas for Circle openings and closings
+ metaphors that illustrate different aspects of the value
+ suggestions for talking pieces and

• lists of questions to initiate multiple passes around the Circle.

The framework we provide shows how a value-centered Circle dialogue might be put together and facilitated.

Formulating Questions

Thought-provoking questions play a critical role in this process. They spur participants to think about values related to their own experiences, using metaphors to link the two. For example, we compare humility (the value) to a seed (a metaphor) to illustrate certain aspects of this value. Then we ask questions that use our knowledge of seeds to help us consider: (a) what humility means for us as a value, and (b) how it has operated in our lives, so that (c) we can consciously practice humility in ways that support our growth. Through the metaphor and some thought-provoking questions, we ground our understanding of humility in our experiences, which in turn helps us practice humility in our lives and relationships.

Questions that build on the metaphors often generate deeper dialogues. Arriving at these questions is not always easy. We find that the more we focus on the concreteness of an image, the more we are able to tap our creative powers in developing questions. For example, when we used the metaphor of a puzzle, we invited each woman to take a puzzle piece, and then all of the women worked together to assemble the puzzle. This exercise stimulated various questions: Which pieces of your life need attention? How will you go about reassembling the pieces of your life? What steps do you need to take to face any addictions or unhealthy relationships or to meet your responsibilities as a parent?

In addition to building on metaphors, questions seem to be most effective when they focus on experiences and invite personal narratives. Those that are more abstract tend not to generate as much dialogue.

Focusing Questions

When questions incorporate issues from everyday life, they allow participants to focus on different aspects of human experience. Which area to focus on is an important decision for Circle keepers; the kinds of questions we posed with the women at the VOARCC reflected the circumstances and desires of the participants as well as the purpose of the Circle. In this guide, the bulk of our questions are intended to help participants deal with their past, face present challenges, and work toward turning their lives around. Accordingly, the questions focus on using the values for personal change.

Depending on the metaphors used in a Circle and the needs of participants, Circle keepers may want to develop questions that focus on other issues. For value-centered Circles held in schools, businesses, churches, or government and professional contexts, participants would most likely respond well to questions that address the issues they face in these environments. How might humility, patience, or any other value help Circle participants function more effectively as teachers, students, businesspeople, lawyers, or public servants? How might a lack of these values create problems?

Encouraging the Active Engagement and Creativity of Participants

As the examples we have given illustrate—transporting a huge box, pulling on a rope, trying to get past a locked door, or assembling a puzzle—activities that dramatize or enact a metaphor take participants to yet deeper levels of dialogue. This is true for many reasons. For one thing, simple physical movement breaks up stuck energy and invites subtle shifts in the group's dynamics when participants sit down. For another, an activity that calls for participants to work together helps to create bonds among them. And doing something—engaging a metaphor in a physical, bodily, tangible way—draws in levels of memory and knowing that are less intellectual and more experiential, less in our heads and more in our lives. An activity may stick in our memory as an image more than words may do. And an activity may elicit responses and emotional reactions more effectively than a simple question may do.

Inviting participants to keep journals, draw pictures, or write stories and poems is also highly effective, because it cultivates our creative, intuitive potentials. In our Circles, we model this activity as equal Circle participants by sharing poems, stories, and other reflective pieces we have written. Poetry in particular can be helpful, because it is all about using word-images to create metaphors for meaning. The point is not to be master poets, artists, or writers but to engage our right brain's holistic powers and to channel these powers in ways that support our growth. Sharing these creative expressions in Circle, if a participant wishes to do so, can be very powerful. The very simplicity and unpolished nature of creative works encourages others to give it a try. Again, the point is not the outcome but the process of expressing ourselves creatively, which is inherently transformative.

Conducting Circles in Institutional Contexts

Since many contexts for using Circles involve going into established institutions (e.g., youth centers, churches, schools, businesses), we want to note the importance of working with the institution and its representatives in planning Circles. As institutions go, few have more stringent rules about the kinds of objects that can be brought inside their facilities than corrections centers.

For the most part, these rules exist for the safety of the residents, so that they cannot hurt each other or themselves. Sharp objects are not permitted in a prison, for example, and this includes not only knives but also paper clips, glass, and wired flowers.

Over time and with consultation with the staff, we learned what we were allowed to bring into the facility. For example, if we wanted to use a bowl, bottle, or vase for our centerpiece or talking piece, we needed to use ones made of plastic instead of glass. With permission, we could bring in a lamp to create a warmer atmosphere, but the lamp had to be made of metal, and we had to be sure that the lightbulb left with us. We also needed permission to use a candle. Our relationship with those who made these decisions helped us understand their concerns and made it easier for us to negotiate how to meet our needs in setting a safe environment for the women in the Circle.

Naturally, it is not necessary to agree with our choices or to use the same metaphors, values, questions, and interpretations that we have used in order to hold a value-centered Circle. It is important that you base your own Circle practices on metaphors and values that are relevant to your participants. Those participating in Circles are the ones to decide what the Circle process needs to include in order to address what is going on in their lives. We do hope that you will find these suggestions useful—even if simply as a springboard for your Circle's own creativity—as you experience the healing power of Circles.

PART 2

Sample Circle Formats

Correlating Values with the Seasons

> The natural world teaches us how to live life in a good way.

To pursue our exploration of values with the women at the VOARCC, we worked with them to identify a set of values that they all shared and that could provide a commonly agreed-upon foundation for the Circle dialogues. The values they chose were ones that were relevant to their lives and experiences. We then helped them find metaphors that in some way illustrated these values. The metaphors needed to be drawn from common ground—things that would be familiar to everyone. For this reason, after the participants identified a set of values that they considered important, we turned to the rhythms of the natural world to find corresponding metaphors—images that could spark their imaginations about these values.

Eventually, we settled on using the seasons and how they are further divided into the months of the year to find metaphors that would help us go deeper into the values. The metaphor of the changing seasons was one that all the women could relate to, especially since many of their sentences lasted one full year. This made the metaphor all the more powerful for many of them. The values explored in this guide reflect, therefore, familiar experiences of the seasonal cycles.

SPRING is the season for cultivating and planting, noticing the sunshine, and embarking on new beginnings. In the spring, seeds take root in the earth; the phase is one of nurturing new growth. Over time and with patient care, the seeds planted in spring develop and gradually fulfill their destiny: they grow into what they are capable of becoming.

Given this overall theme, the three values that we used for our spring Circles were *humility, patience,* and *love.* These values reflect the receptivity and nurturing that spring involves. They prepare us for new beginnings and the rebirth of relationships. They also help us understand each other less judgmentally and more compassionately—with a freer, more expansive, and open spirit. Before we know it, we start applying this same liberating spirit to ourselves. We become more willing to move beyond old hurts, more able to let go of the results of past decisions and actions, and more receptive to new perspectives. Just as nurtured seeds shed their casings, so, too, do our potentials sprout from what is hidden inside us into a fuller and more authentic expression of who we are.

SUMMER is the season of growth and blossoming. The planted seeds rise to the surface, where the sun, wind, and rain help them grow into their full potential. Summer is also a time of preparing for the autumn harvest and the cold of winter. In our summer Circles, we focused on the values of *respect, integrity,* and *courage.* These values are about acknowledging what is coming forth and standing by it—honoring each other's existence and respecting our capacity to "bloom where we're planted." Like a seed, we each have within us an innate attraction to sunshine—to what energizes, warms, and feeds our growth. Living with courage, respect, and integrity expands our capacities to take in these life-giving energies and reflect them. The values engage our natural healing, self-transformative powers, and they protect our growth into whoever and whatever is ours to become.

AUTUMN is the season for harvesting and being nourished by the fruits of the planting. During the harvest time, the earth reveals the abundance of the seed: what the earth received and developed to its fullest is now returned, given back with abundance. The three values we used for our autumn Circles were *generosity*, *forgiveness*, and *gratitude*. Generosity reflects the spirit of the harvest—of sharing in the abundance without fear or defenses. Forgiveness follows naturally. The urges to accuse and punish give way to an appreciation that, with growth and healing, changes in character and relationships become possible that before seemed impossible. The values of generosity and forgiveness expand our internal space, and we are more able to be present with our emotional vulnerability. Accepting our vulnerability is, in a sense, the fruit of our personal harvest, for it paves the way toward living a grateful life. However confusing or conflicted our experiences may have been, a sense of gratitude enables us to embrace them as essential to our growth.

WINTER is the season for planning, dreaming, and storytelling—for reflecting on where we've been, where we're going, and what holds us on a good path. Winter is less outer and more inner—more quiet and contemplative. When the trees lose their leaves, we see what persists beyond change. The seeds persist as well—they "surrender" to their destiny, which for a time gives them the appearance of being lifeless. For our winter Circles, we used the values of *wisdom*, *fortitude*, and *trust*. In this season, we call on wisdom to steady us through long periods of dormancy. We surrender to the cycle and its rhythms, which demand perseverance and fortitude. To cultivate these values, we retreat, step back, and reflect. By relying on values to help us, we gain a sense of trust in movement and change. We trust the process; we trust the values to help us move with it; we trust ourselves more; and we trust our growing capacities to work out our lives in a good way. And so the cycle begins again.

These are the values that the Circle participants at the VOARCC identified as most relevant to their lives. They made sense to us as well, given their correlation to the rhythms of the natural world. Certainly, other groups may identify other values. We focused on these as a good starting point from which to build our Circle processes with the women, because they seemed to be the values that the women came back to again and again.

Spring

I watch as the snow webs melt into Mother Earth,
Our dreams now flow to her.
The water breaks its frozen shell,
Greeting the wind, sun, and sky with ripples and waves.
The crows are gathering in large groups now.
The maples are bleeding sap.

· Excerpt from a poem by Susan Thompson

March

The Value of Humility

The way of humility is to accept life on its terms.

When we say someone is humble, we usually mean that the person is modest and unpretentious; the person realizes his or her place in the larger scheme of things and accepts it. For deeply humble people, this larger scheme is generally understood to be much larger than how social codes may define the parameters of someone's life. Mindful of who they are in the larger scheme of things, those imbued with humility do not try to be other than who they are. Neither do they presume that they know more than others or have a right to impose their views or judgments on others. They tend to listen, observe, and maintain a genuinely open, receptive, and inquiring frame of mind. Besides knowing what they know, they are equally mindful of what they do not know.

Humility can also describe how we rightly feel when we face a new phase or challenge in our lives. We feel humble before something that is new and perhaps overwhelming, as we struggle to understand the magnitude of what lies ahead. Indeed, any beginning can be humble; it is small and not fully formed, full of promise that is not yet realized.

Humility, then, is a value that could well be associated with spring, a time of germination and the earliest beginnings of new growth. Just as a seed germinates under the earth, unseen from our view, so, too, do we often wait in hesitancy and uncertainty of direction before making a change in our lives. For a long time, the new form may not yet appear. Seeds need care to germinate, and, like planted seeds, our resolutions need care and attention. To come to fruition, the seed of any new phase of our lives depends on our determination and willingness to practice humility—a constant mindfulness of where we are in our life's process and a readiness to accept what this involves.

Using a seed as our tangible metaphor for humility, we brought a packet of sunflower seeds to our March Circle. As the talking piece moved several times around the Circle, participants took a seed from the packet and contemplated what the value of humility meant in their lives from various angles. After the third pass of the talking piece, we gathered the seeds and offered to plant them to signify the changes the participants wanted to make in their lives.

What We Used for This Circle

+ A small bowl for the talking piece
+ A packet of sunflower seeds to pass with the talking piece
+ Our basic centerpiece with different seed packets placed around it

Thoughts for the Circle Opening

We all recognize the potential of a seed to become a flower or a vegetable, and we also know that seeds need the proper care and circumstances to break out of their casings and begin their growth. A seed is small and unimpressive, but it holds the potential to bring beauty, sustenance, and power into the world. Seeds depend on water, sun, and tending, while they draw on their own strength and wisdom—their innate biological intelligence—to complete their cycles of growth. Each of these characteristics of seeds can, of course, serve as metaphors for different challenges in human experience as we embark on a new phase of our lives.

The First Pass

Holding the talking piece, we suggested that, like seeds, we have names to identify ourselves and to distinguish ourselves from each other. After speaking about the importance of naming and the meaning of names, we posed some questions:

+ Who named you?
+ What do you know about your name?
+ Do you like your name?
+ Do you have a nickname?

With these questions in mind, we began the first pass. We passed both the bowl as the Circle's talking piece and the packet of seeds from the keeper (one of us) to the left, person by person. When each participant received the bowl and seed packet, she had an opportunity to pick a seed and place it in the bowl and then respond to the questions. After everyone had had a chance to talk (or pass) and put a seed into the bowl, the talking piece and the seed packet came back to the keeper.

The Second Pass

Holding the bowl as the talking piece, we summarized our best sense of what the participants had shared during the first pass. Then we framed the next pass with another set of questions:

+ How might planting and growing a seed tell you something about practicing humility as a value?

+ How might the process of planting seeds and attending to their growth serve as a metaphor for some aspect of your life or some specific experience?
+ How might you apply the value of humility to a situation you currently face?

Again, we passed the bowl and seed packet around the Circle, and each participant had an opportunity to talk about the questions and to choose another seed to put in the bowl.

The Third Pass

After summarizing what was shared in the second pass, we took a third seed from the packet and placed it in the talking-piece bowl. We then posed a third set of questions:

+ Is humility a good value to live by, and if so, why? How does practicing humility help you live in a good way? How does it affect your relationships?
+ What is the opposite of humility? What does it feel like when you are not being humble? Does it help you or hurt you?
+ Considering the metaphor of the seeds, how might the seeds in this bowl relate to your life or to some particular experience you are going through?
+ What type of support do seeds need to grow?
+ What type of support do you need to fulfill your goals or to grow into the kind of person you want to be?

We then began the third pass of the talking piece and the seed packet to the person on our left, inviting the participants to select a third seed, place it in the bowl, and respond to the questions in whatever ways they wished. After everyone had a chance to share, the talking piece and seed packet came back to the keeper, and the third pass was complete.

Thoughts for the Circle Closing

Before passing the talking piece once more around the Circle, we invited the participants to identify one word that would express how living in a humble way might change or support their lives. Later, we planted the seeds, and when they bloomed, we took a photograph of them to share with the participants. We closed the Circle by reading a poem that I (Pat) had written:

> Spring arrives.
> Earth embraces new life in emerging seeds.
> Branches awaken to green buds.
> Sweet simple season
> > To plant,
> > To nourish,
> > To wonder,
> > To dream.

More Metaphors for Humility

Climbing Mountains

In other Circles focusing on humility, we often use the metaphor of three groups of mountain climbers and their differing attitudes toward the climb. A mountain is formidable, and it impacts all the life around it. Clouds, for example, rest on its peaks, and trees and plants hold to its tilt. Myriad forms of life thrive in its crevices and on its cliffs.

Excited with anticipation, the first group of climbers begins planning and preparing for the challenge. They take in the majesty of the mountain, and they realize the enormity of the task ahead. While they may have fears and concerns, they are energized by the promise of the climb. The second group of climbers has a different response. Seeing all the obstacles and risks, they shudder at the prospect of the climb and, despite their desire to reach the summit, they delay getting started because of their fears and self-doubts. Intimidated by the mountain and unable to imagine that they could successfully climb it, the third group never begins at all. They remain paralyzed at the mountain's base. Each group faces the same mountain and the same challenge, yet each group's response to the mountain is different.

What enables the first group to move, while the second and third groups either hesitate or don't move at all? The answer lies in three different concepts of humility. The humility of the first group fosters care and attention to the task ahead. Humble in the face of the challenge, these climbers embrace the mountain with respect and move cautiously and realistically toward the goal, mindful of where they are and the magnitude of the task they face.

For groups two and three, by contrast, humility functions as a cover for fears, doubts, and insecurities. They are impeded, in fact, by their confusion about what it means to be humble—a confusion that can become paralyzing: e.g., "I can't do it, so why try?" or "I'm not good enough, so I'm unworthy of following this path." Humility as a value is not, however, debilitating but empowering. Far from being synonymous with low self-esteem or self-denigration, humility involves a full appreciation of who we are that holds in balance our strengths and our weaknesses. We can be truly effective only when we balance an awareness of what we know and are capable of doing with an equal awareness of what we do not know and have not yet mastered.

Metaphorically, if there is a mountain that is ours to climb, how might the value of humility help us? For example, might overcoming challenges mean forcing ourselves onto a situation and "making" things happen? This would be arrogance, not humility. Would it mean giving ourselves over to fears or pride that would have us "camp out" inside ourselves, rendering us unable to move or change? This would be self-rejecting and self-defeating. Instead, by helping us develop an honest appreciation of who we are, humility makes it easier for us to call on our strengths when we need them as well as to reach out for help when we need that too. With humility, we can assess what needs to be done and call on our practical, self-aware mind to guide our steps in making it happen.

Whenever we have used the mountain metaphor to facilitate dialogue about humility, we have brought pictures of mountains to serve as the Circle's centerpiece. Using a rock as the talking piece to symbolize the mountain and the hard core of our challenges, we have posed such questions as the following:

+ What story do you tell yourself when you face a personal challenge?
+ How do you approach dealing with a personal challenge?
+ What values do you bring to meeting your challenges?
+ How might the value of humility assist you in dealing with some of the current challenges in your life?

Melting Ice

Although solid, ice can readily become fluid, for it yields to heat and pressure. Using a centerpiece of colored ice cubes to signify diversity in culture, knowledge, skills, interests, and experiences and a cup of water as a talking piece, we invited the participants to reflect on how they have been fluid—or not—when they have faced personal challenges. We then posed some questions:

+ What different approaches have you used to respond to challenges that seem hard and impassable? Which responses tend to work, and which don't?

+ How might being flexible make you more effective and bring out your strengths when you deal with challenges?
+ How might the value of humility assist you in dealing with an apparently fixed, rigid, or intractable situation?
+ How might practicing humility strengthen your self-esteem?

Blowing Glass

Bending to heat and the design of the artist, blown glass can be molded into exquisite forms. Its hardness and brittleness melt away, enabling the glass to be shaped. Engaging this metaphor to explore humility and its power to bring beauty and grace into our lives, we have used a centerpiece of flowers placed in a blown glass vase and a talking piece of blown glass jewelry (or, as we mentioned earlier, a plastic vase and plastic jewelry if the Circle is being held in a corrections facility). These Circles explored how humility might give us the willingness to melt, bend, and change when we come up against obstacles and apparently impossible situations. Serving as the Circle keepers, we framed multiple rounds with some questions:

+ With a challenge you currently face in mind, how might being willing to "melt and bend" make it easier for you to go forward with change?
+ How could practicing humility help you transform a difficult situation into a situation that holds promise and possibilities that you may not have recognized before?
+ How might practicing humility help you transform a challenge that you currently face into something positive—something you might even appreciate and admire?

April

The Value of Patience

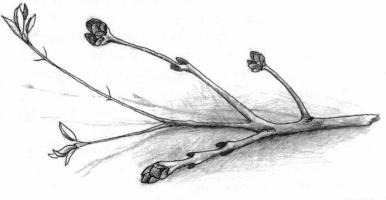

Patience involves trusting the order of growth—
its rhythm, power, wisdom, and goodness.

In a group of people, listening and not interrupting take patience. During the Circle process, only one person speaks at a time. By learning to be patient with each other in how we tell our stories and express ourselves, Circle participants come to appreciate, understand, and identify with each other. In a similar way, observing our own lives with patience enables us to see and hear things about ourselves that we may have otherwise missed.

Living life patiently reveals these subtleties, and observing the seasonal cycles often inspires the patience we need. For example, the slow melting of snow reveals the buds of spring; the lingering moments of summer make space for relaxation; the changing colors of autumn prepare us for the harvest; and the slumber and solitude of winter hold us in reflection, while we gather energy for the birth that follows. Patience is the way of the natural world, and practicing patience attunes us with the natural rhythm and gradual unfolding of our lives.

Patience is essential to our life's journey because growth takes time; it does not happen all at once. No matter what kind of growth we are considering—the growth of a child, a mind, heart, or soul, a friendship, a marriage, a family, a career, a community, or a society—growth takes the time it takes. It can't be rushed. We can't make a baby ready for college. We can't rectify centuries of harms and injustices with quick fixes, any more than we can heal from decades of abusive relationships overnight. Life processes such as healing, transformation, and growth unfold at their own pace and according to their own dynamics. Patience is about embracing these natural rhythms and moving with them, without trying to rush or force things.

To help keep the natural rhythm in view and to fortify our trust in patience, we can remember the growth patterns we have experienced over the course of our lives. Just as the yearly rings of a tree mark its growth cycles, so, too, are our cycles of growth marked by events, accomplishments, and memories. We can remember times when we desperately wanted things to move more quickly, yet looking back, we probably see why they needed the time they did. In fact, we may now wish they had lasted longer. Patience helps us trust that something good is going on—something to do with natural growth. If we slow down and take our time, we will more likely appreciate the good going on and not wish it to pass too quickly.

Once again, being in Circle is definitely a lesson in patience. One young VOARCC participant commented, "I quieted down, slowed down." At first, people can't wait for the talking piece to come to them. But with time, they appreciate the measured pace. They stop rehearsing in their heads what they want to say and instead relax into hearing what others are saying. They experience what it is to listen, and this cultivates patience. The young woman added, "I truly benefited from coming to the talking Circle."

What We Used for This Circle

+ An arrangement of pieces of tree bark as the centerpiece
+ A budding tree bough for a talking piece
+ A closing gift of decorative leaves

Thoughts for the Circle Opening

A tree's age is reflected in its rings. If the tree did not grow and change each year, it would die, and no new rings would form. Natural growth is inherently slow and, in that sense, provides a useful metaphor for patience; natural processes continue steadily, quietly, moment by moment over time.

Patience aligns us with the slowness of natural growth. Practicing this value helps us attend to life's cycles without upset and with trust in the natural process. We develop patience, for example, when we care for an elder, teach a child, nurse the sick, sit with the dying, work through life changes, or struggle against racism, oppression, and injustice. We also learn about patience when we engage in relationships and work through the challenges that go with them. Relationships have their own seasons and cycles, and patience gives us the strength to appreciate these natural rhythms and move with them. Here are some of the questions we raised as we pondered patience as a value:

+ Do we need patience in our lives? If so, why? How does it help us?
+ What rewards come from practicing patience? How might patience make our lives better?

+ Why is practicing patience considered a sign of strength in a person?
+ How might being patient make us more aware of personal boundaries?

The First Pass

Before passing the talking piece, I (Pat) read another poem that I had written:

Gazing from my window
At the snow-streaked yard,
I notice the slashed stump of a broken tree
Silhouetted in the light of dawn.

I pondered its purpose at this moment,
The string of events that led to this place.

What determined its destiny,
        Its presence as a stump
            Beneath the window
            In my yard?

Few will notice
Or inquire about its beauty
The fullness it once had,
In a life now past.

Yet there in my yard,
It has a new reason to exist:
    Simple,
        Uncomplicated,
            Different from before.

Questions for the First Pass

+ Describe two recent events or experiences in your life that were significant.
+ How long did it take to prepare for these events or to create these experiences?
+ How have these events or experiences—and the process by which they came into existence—been important to your growth?

Questions for the Second Pass

+ What situation in your life took time to understand, forgive, mend, or bring to a resolution?
+ Why did that situation take time, and did you need patience to see it through?
+ If you needed patience, what did it feel like to practice it? Was it difficult? Why? What makes patience difficult for you?
+ How did you maintain a patient response?
+ What happened if you became impatient?

Questions for the Third Pass

+ Until our next Circle, how might you practice patience more mindfully in your life?
+ What experiences in the upcoming days, weeks, months, or year might require that you consciously exercise patience?
+ What have you learned about patience that might help you practice it more consistently and from an inner place?

Thoughts for the Circle Closing

We made our final comments as keepers, summarizing what the participants had shared about patience from their lives. We then presented each participant with a closing gift of a leaf, saying to each person:

> "Receive this leaf as a symbol of the patient journey
> of your life."

More Metaphors for Patience

Assembling a Jigsaw Puzzle

Some people see a jigsaw puzzle as a challenge, while others look at it as a worthless endeavor. Putting together a one-thousand-piece jigsaw puzzle takes time, but it is not impossible and the experience can be a lesson in patience. Each puzzle piece is within reach, and each is right for a given spot. Yet how all the pieces fit together is not obvious; in fact, the pieces look like a jumbled, disjointed mess. We have to go slowly and look at all the pieces, perhaps sorting them by color or image. Trying to rush the process does not help, yet the puzzle will not come together if we give up and walk away either. Assembling the puzzle is a slow process, but with patience, a whole image emerges. As it does, the process becomes easier. We begin to get the hang of where the pieces might fit.

Like an unassembled jigsaw puzzle, a personal dilemma may seem impossible to figure out, and we may choose to walk away and give up on the challenge altogether. Yet dilemmas in life can be resolved, even though it may take time and patience to find the right pieces and put them together. Patience is about being willing to work toward a solution—slow as it may be in coming—rather than being overcome with impatience because the problem seems so hard, demands so much, or does not yield readily. Patience is about waiting for a new picture to emerge and trusting the growth process at work. With time and patience, a dilemma can be transformed. Difficulty gives way to opportunity, failure to success, and loss to gain.

When we used the metaphor of a puzzle in our Circles, we invited people to consider some questions: What insights might we gain if we approach the dilemmas in our lives as jigsaw puzzles that we have yet to assemble? And what might the jigsaw puzzle metaphor tell us about patience?

To pursue these questions, we created our own jigsaw puzzle out of blank paper which, when assembled, spelled the word *patience*. We placed the jumble of pieces in the middle as the Circle's centerpiece, and we used one piece of the puzzle as the talking piece. Before the Circle began, we discussed how our lives unfold in many unexpected, unforeseen, and often perplexing ways, and how each person and experience in our lives holds a piece of our life's puzzle. Practicing patience has to do with allowing ourselves and others the time we need to discover how all the pieces come together in a meaningful way.

With each pass around the Circle, we invited participants to take a puzzle piece from the center when the talking piece came to them and to imagine what the puzzle would look like when it was finally assembled. After three passes, the participants held all the puzzle pieces, and we invited them to put the puzzle together. The word "patience" soon emerged. We then posed some questions:

+ What surprised you about the process of assembling the puzzle and its result?
+ What did it feel like to work together on assembling this puzzle, and what role did patience play in the process?
+ How might consciously practicing patience alter your approach to your life?

+ How might practicing patience affect your sense of yourself?
+ How would your life be different if patience were not part of your approach? For example, how would impatience affect how you live and the choices you make? How would it affect your relationships?
+ How might patience help you as you put together your life's puzzle day by day?

The Passage of Time

A day does not end before sunset, and the sun does not set until the day is complete. Regardless of how our days go, the setting sun always waits at the end. Its setting does not linger if our day has gone well, nor does it set sooner if our day has been a challenge. The sun cannot be hurried or slowed down. Accordingly, we have to adjust our pace, thoughts, and activities to the passage of time—though we don't necessarily find this easy to do—because time lies beyond our control.

To develop this metaphor, we put together a centerpiece of images of sunrises and sunsets to represent the passage of time and used an hourglass as the talking piece. We then invited participants to reflect on the passage of a day as a metaphor for living our lives with patience. We asked, for instance:

+ What does the passage of time suggest about the role of patience in your life?
+ Do you need to practice patience in your life? If you feel that you do, what does practicing patience contribute to how you approach your life? How do you feel when you bring patience to a situation?
+ When you are faced with a dilemma, how could being patient support the resolution of things?

+ How might patience help you deal with disappointment or grief?
+ What would your life be like if you did not practice patience? How would it look and feel different?

Waiting for Water to Boil

Waiting for water to boil provides another familiar metaphor that can be used to talk about patience. Once we turn the heat on "High," nothing we do further will accelerate the process, and if we try to make the water boil faster, it will seem to take even longer. Sometimes simply waiting is what patience requires. Just as we must wait for water to reach its boiling point, we sometimes have to wait for something to manifest in our lives. In these situations, trying to rush or force things to happen will most likely backfire and make the process seem even longer. Practicing patience often means allowing a situation to reach its own natural or logical conclusion. Yet such acceptance also means being willing to set aside our egos and concepts of how and when things should work out. Patience provides the perspective needed for this, and as we embrace this acceptance, we invite Spirit—that which is beyond all of us but which includes the good of us all—to influence the outcome.

To reinforce this metaphor, we used a bowl of water and two candles, representing liquid and heat, as a centerpiece and a stone with the word "patience" written or engraved on it as a talking piece. We then posed some questions:

+ When dealing with challenges, conflicts, or dilemmas in your life, at what point does patience influence how things work out? Where does patience come in?
+ Have there been situations in your life where you could have been more patient? If so, how did impatience

affect your experience, and how might practicing more patience have helped?

+ If patience is a virtue—something good in our lives that benefits us and those around us—why is it so hard to be patient? Why is it a way of being that we have to learn and remind ourselves to practice? What has been hardest for you to learn about being patient?

+ Are there times when it's better not to be patient? If so, when is it time to be patient and when is it time to step in, intervene, and act? How do you decide which to do when?

May

The Value of Love

Love lived well
creates a community
of lasting connection
and care.

When we speak of love, we think of compassion, caring, tenderness, and connection, born of an abiding commitment to the
well-being of both ourselves and others. Love encompasses other
qualities as well: trust, surrender, sacrifice, wonder, belief, con-
tentment, and hope. To love is to be steadfastly generous, supportive, and authentic in all our relations. "All our relations" is the
key, and the relation that is sometimes most overlooked is the
one we have with ourselves. Yet it is hard to love others if we do
not love ourselves as well. Holding ourselves in a loving way expands our capacities to experience love, because then love flows
freely through all our relationships. Loving ourselves enables
us to receive the love of others—family members, friends, and
sweethearts. We do not selectively filter or even block the love
they express.

When love flows freely, communities form. This often happens naturally in ongoing Circle programs, such as the one we
held at the VOARCC. The women opened up in the Circles and
shared from their hearts about their lives and struggles. Over
time, they experienced a sense of nonjudgmental acceptance

and support from each other as members of a community. One woman said, "The Circle gives me positive energy and a chance to feel a part of a family. . . . While in Circle, I feel a closeness and a spiritual warmth." Another woman expressed similar feelings: "The Circle was a positive experience and reminded me that I am a part of a community. I felt close with the other Circle participants. I felt love and joy in that moment, and I know that love is the answer to whatever I need to face in my life."

> "In Circle, I felt an inner peace that I have not felt for a long while. I felt a self-love that was a missing piece in my life. The Circle experience made me comfortable with my feelings and with expressing my feelings."
>
> –Circle participant incarcerated at the VOARCC

Feeling the genuine love and support of others, the participants dared to feel that they were lovable, and they began to take the first steps toward accepting and loving themselves. "The Circle experience showed me how to be a better person," one woman commented, "and how to love myself." Another woman spoke of her increased capacity to love and accept herself and to recognize the inner peace that goes with this inner shift.

For those who wanted to maintain their spiritual lives while incarcerated, we also explored how love can be experienced through the unseen presence of the Creator. From a spiritual perspective, we assume that we each have our place in an unfolding story that has meaning and purpose. To support this sense, we have often shared Susan Thompson's piece "A Story for My Sisters" to convey the inclusiveness of love—its power not only to support the good in our lives but also to call forth our innate powers of healing and self-transformation.

A Story for My Sisters

One day while observing Earth, the Creator noticed a particular place where prayers were streaming forth with great intensity. Taking a closer look, the Creator saw that the prayers were coming from the middle of the continent called North America. Looking even closer, the prayers were coming from a place called Minnesota—Mni Sota Makoce, the term that the land's Original People, the Dakota, have called it since time immemorial. Looking closer yet, the prayers were coming from a brick building standing between two cemeteries. As the Creator brought the building into view, a sign appeared in front of it: Volunteers of America Regional Corrections Center. The Creator then spoke with the wingeds and the four-leggeds who lived nearby and asked them about all the prayers flowing from that place.

The wingeds and the four-leggeds replied, "Creator, we see sisters, mothers, daughters, and grandmothers in there. The women are at crossroads in their lives. They were removed from situations that were harmful to others and to themselves. They send their prayers with great intensity now, because they have been holding on to their prayers and not sending them for so long." The Creator could see that the women were locked up and in great need. For too long they had been trying to climb mountains on their own without reaching out to the Creator for help. They did not realize until now that if they kept a channel of prayer open to the Creator, the Creator would find them.

The Creator then decided to go inside the building and look around. In each woman's face was the Creator's reflection. Seeing each face, the Creator understood what had happened to each woman and what each woman desired most in her heart. Taking in the entire picture, the Creator said, "My other children in North America need these women. These women carry the potential of all my gifts. How can I help them understand their importance and how much they are needed to help their sisters and brothers become free from addictions and obsessions?" A plan to help them formed in the mind of the Creator.

The Creator called the Guides of the women to Counsel and said: "As of now, I will give you greater power of protection. Starting now, the women will be able to see the signs that you give them. As of today, I will forgive all that has come before. These women have caused hurt, because they have suffered great hurt. Today we start fresh. All contracts binding them to hurts of the past are dissolved. I will tell them to start where they stand and make a circle for healing. From there, they are instructed to spiral out as needed, not forgetting to come back to you as their Guides to check in. Each one will learn her obligations to herself. I recommend prayers for their guidance. Tell them to watch for my signs, for they will be subtle, quiet, and natural to each one's life. My signs will show the women how to build new lives. This is the way we shall proceed." The Counsel ended, and the Creator and the Guides went their ways.

The women in the brick building never knew the Creator had been with them, but soon they noticed changes. They began to see events in their lives coming together in good ways, as their Guides worked to support the plan of the Creator. To this day, the women have a sense of their Guides with them, and the channels between them and their Guides remain open. Each day their Guides work hard to show the women how to implement the Creator's great plan for them and to help them remember that guidance and support are only a request away.

Paula Daine reinforces this story's message of unseen guidance based on her experiences as a Michigan Métis Chippewa Circle keeper: "The Great Spirit often sends us helpers in the forms of his creation: flyers, four-leggeds, swimmers, crawlers, rock people. The medicine or essence of this being we experience is often a metaphor for what we most need at the time."

What We Used for This Circle

- A centerpiece of rose petals scattered around a vase of red roses set on a yellow cloth
- A single rose for a talking piece
- A closing gift of an artificial rosebud for each participant

Thoughts for the Circle Opening

We chose a rose as a metaphor for love, not only because it is such a widespread cultural symbol for love, but also because the rose blooms with beauty in spite of its thorns. Indeed, this is probably why roses became so popular as a symbol for love. Metaphorically, the thorns on a rose stem suggest that love blossoms as we face challenges, pain, fear, and rejections. Love—real love, not the romance fantasy—is not only "a bed of roses," it is also a bed of thorns. To love is to embrace each other's vulnerabilities, fears, and weak points, neither pretending these elements aren't there nor trying to run away from them. Love and the realities of pain exist side by side, since both are part of life.

Practicing the value of love helps us respond to hard or painful experiences not by shutting down our feelings but by keeping our hearts open. To do this, love engages other values—such as understanding, forgiveness, compassion, humility, and patience— as the context or container in which to hold our relationships, especially in thorny times. Responding to the thorns of hurt and pain through our best values, we keep love "blooming" as a trusted, constant reality in our lives. Love is not, therefore, about having no pain but about persisting in expressing love in the midst of pain—with thorns all around.

This does not mean that love asks us to endure abuse. Tolerating abusive behavior does not express love, either to ourselves or to the abuser. Love can be difficult at times, to say the least, and drawing the line at addictive or abusive behavior is often the most loving action we can take. Here again, the metaphor of a rose applies. Like a rose, our love can be both full of tenderness and sharply effective in setting boundaries to protect our good, the good of those we love, and the good of our relationships. Thorns exist, after all, to protect the rose. Because love's path includes joy and pain, flowers and thorns, practicing love as a value is not easy, yet love is also why we are here and it is what keeps us going.

We began the Circle by playing the song "The Rose" by Bette Midler as the Circle's opening. We posed some general questions to open the dialogue, knowing that participants may choose to raise other aspects of their experiences with love or may not be ready to speak about love at all.

Questions for the First Pass

+ What does the metaphor "love is a rose" mean to you?
+ How is love manifested in your life today?
+ How does your life change when the value of love is expressed and present?
+ What has been the most powerful experience of love in your life?
+ How do you protect the flow of love in your life? What other ways of protecting love might be effective?
+ When has love meant drawing your boundaries— showing your thorns?
+ How have you responded to others when they felt a need to assert their thorns?

Questions for the Second Pass

+ Do you feel love for yourself? How does that feel?
+ When in your life have you felt loved by others?
+ How have you experienced love over the course of your

life? Has it felt like mostly flowers or mostly thorns?
Why might this be so?

+ In what situation today might you be able to show love
  to another person?
+ How do you feel when you express love to someone else?
+ How do you feel when you receive love from another?
  Does it feel natural to you or difficult?
+ In what situation today might you allow yourself to
  receive love from another?

Question for the Third Pass

+ In what ways can you express love to yourself, your
  family, your friends, or your community? In what ways
  are you able to receive love from them?
+ What makes expressing love easy and natural for you?
+ What makes expressing love difficult?
+ When expressing love seems difficult, which qualities
  or values help you to approach others with an open
  heart?

Thoughts for the Circle Closing

After summarizing what the participants had shared about their
experiences with love, we presented each participant with a closing gift of an artificial rosebud, saying:

> Receive this rosebud as a symbol of the fullness of your jour-
> ney with love through your life. Embrace all that love offers
> you, whether in thorns or in beauty. Know that everything
> is connected and that all life has meaning. Let go of whatever
> diminishes your love of who you are and your love for others.
> Be gentle with yourself, for love always brings lessons to be
> learned.

More Metaphors for Love

Hands

Often, body language communicates as clearly as words, and the language of our hands speaks of giving and receiving. We greet with our hands, pray with our hands, and play with our hands. We comfort, heal, work, and serve with our hands. In this giving and receiving, we create a sense of balance and harmony, and in this balanced flow, love moves through our lives. We can use our hands to nurture in other ways as well, such as planting gardens, cooking, and serving food. When the opportunity comes, we offer a helping hand. In these instances, our hands tell the stories of our hearts.

Whenever we used the hand as a metaphor for love, we asked participants to trace their hands on a piece of colored paper. The participants then put the traced hands in a bowl, which served as the Circle's centerpiece; it symbolized for us the unity of love. We often used a picture of two hands holding a heart as a talking piece for this Circle. As it was passed hand to hand around the Circle, we suggested that the participants spend a moment observing their hands. As they did this, we raised some questions:

- What do you observe about your hands?
- How do your hands feel?
- How have you recently used your hands to express love toward another person?
- How might you use your hands to support yourself through a personal challenge?

Heart

The heart is, of course, another traditional symbol of love. Ultimately, the love of the Creator is expressed to us through the gift of life, and so with each beat of our hearts, we are reminded that we have been given this gift. A "warm-hearted" person is a loving person, while a person with a "closed heart" is someone who is fearful and in emotional pain. If we tell someone to "have a heart," we are imploring the person to act with compassion, forgiveness, or understanding. If we tell someone to "take heart," we are pointing to the rose in the midst of thorns.

To reinforce this metaphor, we used a bowl of candy hearts as a centerpiece to represent the individual heart of each participant and a glass (or plastic) heart as the talking piece. We then posed some questions:

+ How would you describe your heart in relation to your loved ones?
+ What situation or challenge in your life has recently tempted you to close your heart or shut yourself off from love?
+ When you feel emotional pain, which is the most healing response: To close your heart or to open your heart? To make your heart harder or softer? To become more defensive or more receptive?
+ Why might it be true that "an open heart is a happy heart"?
+ What situation that you face today might change if you opened your heart?

A Burning Candle

The softly burning flame of a candle is another rich metaphor for the flicker of love in the human heart. A candle's flame can be easily extinguished and depends on the watchful eye of its tender to keep burning. A loving heart can be just as vulnerable. A burning candle contributes to an atmosphere of softness, balance, and centeredness that most people find soothing and restful. So, too, an open heart welcomes those around it, calms us, and allays our fears.

Using a tall candleholder and a lit candle as the centerpiece and an unlit candle as the talking piece, we posed various questions to help participants reflect on this age-old metaphor for love:

- What does the metaphor of a burning candle suggest about love as a value in your life?
- How do you tend love and keep its flame alive?
- What experiences have challenged you to express more love as a means to light your path through troubled times in a relationship?
- As you reflect on love, can you recall a situation in which, by expressing a greater loving vulnerability, you could have brought warmth and lightened things up?
- How might expressing love transform a painful or difficult situation and light the way out of impasse?

Summer

I see the wild berries on their ripening journey,
Subtle fireflies sparkle in the short summer nights.
Burdock growing in a crack of cement,
Mullein sprouting up along the roadside,
Owl singing its night song in the distance.

· *Excerpt from a poem by Susan Thompson*

June

The Value of Respect

My friend, I accept you.
My friend, I believe you.
My friend, I love you.
My friend, for you I hold respect.

My prayer is that you accept yourself.
My prayer is that you believe in yourself.
My prayer is that you love yourself.
My prayer is that you honor yourself
As your Creator honors you:
In strength, in vulnerability,
In joy, and in sorrow.

To respect others means to hold them in esteem, to honor their uniqueness, and to treat them with dignity. Respect acknowledges that we are each different and that our very uniqueness makes us needed within the whole. Each of us has something to contribute, and we each need the contributions of others for our lives to be rich and our world whole. All of creation, therefore, warrants our appreciation and respect, and we are likewise called to respect and honor ourselves.

Our societies have unfortunately conditioned some of us to perceive others as "the Other." "Other-izing" turns fellow beings into objects as a way of diminishing them on a supposed hierarchy of life. The "less than" status can then be used to justify exploiting one group for the benefit of another. Once a group has been accorded "less than" status based on some perceived set of differences, their gifts and unique contributions are not honored, neither are their rightful boundaries respected. Differences are used as a reason to divide, exploit, and oppress people.

Other-izing on the basis of differences perpetuates violence and injustice, because it does not honor as sacred the core of another's existence as an autonomous, living being—an "I," not an "it." In contrast to the Euro-American pattern of according respect only to a narrow subset of humans, Indigenous cultures by and large accord unconditional respect to all who share their world with us. The universe is filled with an incredible diversity of beings, all of whom deserve the respect that is due an "I." It is, after all, to them that we owe our continued existence.

To put this in terms used by many Indigenous Peoples, practicing respect calls us to acknowledge all beings as our relatives. Everything in the universe is related, and we depend on each other. Being respectful as a way of life means holding a space of deep regard for others and staying mindful of how we can nourish all our relations by being good relatives to each other.

Circles are one place where we can experience how respect feels, since the value of respect is integral to the Circle process. Giving and receiving respect become completely natural among participants. Many Circle keepers identify respect as the single most important value that Circles both require and instill. Participating in Circles involves spending most of our time listening. We take in others' words and feelings quietly and without judgment. We show respect. When it is our turn to speak, we receive respect from the other participants as well.

Examining this value during June has its logic. In June, the light reaches its peak in the northern hemisphere. All that appeared asleep months ago is now abundantly awake. It is summer, the season of growth. We need only walk outside and see the burgeoning plant and animal life to respect the incredible diversity of the natural world and appreciate that each being contributes something distinct to the whole.

Respect also involves being aware of the balance between vulnerability and strength. To respect another's different and unique qualities is to acknowledge our limitations as well—that we are not all things. We are the age we are and not another age; we are a certain gender and of a specific culture and ancestry; we look and behave as we do and not another way; we have our own experiences, but not the experiences of others. Acknowledging and respecting our limits has a positive effect on us and our relationships, because it makes us humble and respectful of others.

Indeed, respect begins with recognizing the boundaries that mark another's uniqueness. It then calls us to be humble before those differences (humility), patient with them (patience), and accepting of their boundaries (love). Another's differences need not feel threatening, as if they diminish us, but can be a source of strength and joy, because our world is richer for them. The fact that we are all here *and* different is a good thing. We discover that we have more than ourselves to turn to for help. Practicing respect for our very differences builds our life-support systems.

June is a month that reflects these dynamics—diversity, vulnerability, and strength. Nature often feels soft and new at this time. However, June can also bring tornadoes, flooding, and other fierce weather. Using this as a metaphor, who hasn't experienced both soft periods and whirlwinds? Both get our attention. Just as we honor both the tenderness and the power of nature in June, so, too, practicing respect involves honoring each others' strengths and weaknesses. Beyond merely "tolerating" differences, respect embraces them. Again, without the differences among us, we could not survive.

Because differences are fundamental to life, the value of respect urges us to practice respect categorically and inclusively. In this sense, respect and love work together. Practicing respect is about receiving others as they are—unconditionally. Love then deepens our appreciation of others, which naturally reinforces respect.

As much as respect is good to practice, though, it is not necessarily easy to do. What may seem respectful in some situations may be disrespectful in others. For example, do we show respect by approaching or distancing ourselves from a person or situation? Depending on the circumstances, either choice could be respectful. Approaching conveys a desire to engage; distancing conveys a desire to respect boundaries and another's need for space. The more we practice respect, the easier it is to make these calls.

We have typically used a feather as our metaphor for respect. In many cultures, the structure and beauty of feathers fascinate people and inspire awe. Feathers can have many colors, and the fine filaments on the quill vary in length and quality. Some are soft and downy, while others are stiffer. Feathers blend differences together into a united form that carries birds thousands of miles in the air. If feathers were all the same shape, or if the filaments on a feather were all of the same size and texture, birds could not fly. The physics of feathers teaches the value of differences and why respect among differences is essential.

But what does respecting differences look like? How does it feel? What does disrespect look and feel like? Drawing on personal experiences, Circle participants generally have much to share about respect as a value.

What We Used for This Circle

+ A centerpiece consisting of a bowl of feathers to represent respect and two candles to represent the connection between respect and love

+ A single feather for the talking piece
+ A closing gift of a feather from the centerpiece

Thoughts for the Circle Opening

To open a Circle focused on respect, we like to read the story of "The Ugly Feather" from the book *Peacemaking Circles*. The story is about what happened in a Circle for a young man who had gotten into trouble. It is also about what it means to be good relatives to each other, which in turn is about practicing respect.

The Ugly Feather

Slumped in his chair, legs stretched out, arms folded and head down, Jamie listened as the feather was passed around the Circle. People were talking about him and his crime. He heard anger, but mostly he heard people asking him in many different ways: Why? Why had he spent so many years lost to alcohol and crime? When was he going to change? What would it take for him to change? Did he not care about the people he hurt? He was now twenty-one; when was he going to grow up? When was he going to take responsibility for his life?

Amidst the questions and anger were comments reflecting on his past—about the good things he had done. Some spoke about how he dealt with elders and young people and about what he could be. These comments surprised him. Those were the only times he looked up. A furtive glance at those who spoke kindly about him briefly altered his otherwise frozen posture, sending messages that he didn't care and perhaps wasn't even listening.

But Jamie was listening. He was nervous, very nervous. He knew the feather would soon be passed to him. Soon he would have to talk and answer some questions. In court, anger, hostility, and a silent resignation to the process enabled him to slip through without being involved. Not there.

The feather came to him. He held the feather, twirling it in his hands. He paused. "I don't know what to say. I'm here because I want to change. That's it."

He passed the feather to John with a desperate hope that John might answer all the questions. John, a respected elder, had been talking with him for weeks, trying to help him prepare for the Circle. John was in the Circle to support him. Jamie thought John would help him now.

John held the feather but didn't speak. Jamie worried that John might pass the feather back to him. John reached into his pouch and pulled out another feather. This feather was hardly recognizable as an eagle feather. It was twisted and large gaps suggested strands were missing. It was bedraggled, unkempt, and obviously not cared for—not a sacred object. John held up the feather for everyone to see.

"This is a very ugly feather. I don't know when I've seen such an ugly feather. This feather reminds me of when I was running wild and crazy. I was missing many strands, it seemed. I was twisted up inside, full of booze and anger, full of not caring for anyone, not even for myself. I was an ugly feather with lost gaps in my life. I want everyone to see up close how ugly this feather really is, so I'm going to pass it around while I talk. Hold this feather for a while. Look at it, feel it, and see how ugly and un-cared for it is."

As the feather passed around the Circle, John spoke about his youth and broken life. . . .

By the time John finished the story of his youth, the old, ugly feather had been around the Circle. Jamie held it for a moment, stroked it, and passed it to John. Holding up the old feather, John said, "Now, look how beautiful this old, ugly feather has become."

The feather was different. Maybe not beautiful, but certainly not ugly. Everyone, as they held the feather and listened to John, had stroked it almost unconsciously, as most of us do when holding a feather.

Still holding up the feather, John said, "This feather is like me. Once I was ugly, mad, and twisted up by anger. There were big gaps in my life. Many important parts of living a good life were missing. Then Agnes and several others came into my life. They held me, cared for me, and changed me like this feather. That's what we all have to do with Jamie. If all of us touch him with caring hands, we can help him become like this feather. Everything is beautiful, is sacred. It takes caring to bring out beauty, to make someone realize they are sacred, and to make us realize they are sacred. So I'm asking all of us tonight to touch Jamie's life, to care for him, to bring out his beauty, his sacred spirit."

John spoke about how Jamie had come to him asking for help. They had spoken several times . . . and told each other the stories of their lives. "I believe in this young man. I believe he is genuine about wanting to change. In our old ways, we give a feather to those we believe in, those we want to know the teachings."

John stood, called upon Jamie to stand up, and presented Jamie with the once-ugly feather. "Jamie, this feather is yours. It says to you we believe in you. As this feather has been changed into something beautiful by the caring hands of everyone in the Circle, so will you be touched by the caring hands of all the people in our community. By respecting yourself, you will respect those who touch your life with care. Respect this feather. Let it keep you aware of what you are and of how people care about you."

Questions for the First Pass

+ If you were a feather, how would you want to be treated? What does the metaphor of holding a feather convey to you about practicing respect?
+ How have you been "held" in your life? Who has shown

you respect? How did their respectful treatment of you make you feel?

+ When have you not been treated respectfully? By whom? What did that experience of disrespect feel like?

+ What level of respect do you now have for yourself? Where did this respect come from?

+ How do you express respect—or disrespect—for yourself?

Questions for the Second Pass

+ How important for you is respect as a value? What role does this value have in your life?

+ How did you first learn about respecting yourself and others?

+ What level of respect do you have for the people and situations in your life? Why?

+ How do you express this respect or lack of respect?

+ What might change if you practiced respect in these areas—if you "held" these areas of your life in respect-ful ways? What would it mean to do this?

+ Do you feel you have gained the respect of your family, friends, and community? If not, how would you go about gaining their respect?

+ Is the respect of family, friends, and community impor-tant for you to have? Why?

The Third Pass

After we summarized what the participants had shared during the second pass, we invited participants to comment on what they had experienced as well. Following the summary, we picked up the bowl of small feathers and invited the Circle participants to select a feather from the bowl. We then asked the participants:

+ Why did you pick the feather that you selected?
+ What will you do with the feather?
+ What do you think is the story behind the feather you are now holding?
+ When you hold this feather in the future, what will it bring to your mind?

Thoughts for the Circle Closing

After summarizing what was shared, we noted that the simple gift of a bird's feather could serve as a reminder to everyone present to express respect to ourselves and to others as we go about our lives between now and the next Circle. We then read some closing words:

> Feathers everywhere dot the grass, left by geese on their
> flight back from the south. I pick one up and hold it. It is
> delicate and soft. It is a gift. Carefully, I carry it with me.
> Later, I respectfully place it with my other gifts
> from nature.

More Metaphors for Respect

Weather Gauge

Watching weather reports and responding to weather predictions are everyday occurrences. If we "respect" the changing weather, we can most likely avoid a host of difficulties. We dress in warm clothes in the winter so we don't get frostbite; we arrange our schedules so we don't drive during an ice storm or blizzard; and we use sunscreen, especially when the sun is high, so we don't get sunburned. In the midst of a thunderstorm, we don't stand outside and yell "Stop!" or pretend it isn't happening; we go inside. And we prepare for tornadoes, hurricanes, and other weather disasters as best we can.

In other words, we respect weather changes and adapt ourselves accordingly. Similarly, the changes people go through are not ours to control. Just as we watch the weather for patterns of change, so, too, can we watch for patterns of change in ourselves and in others. Noticing changes, we can respond appropriately, respectfully.

The metaphor we chose to help focus these aspects of respect is the weather gauge, a tool for tracking the weather. To practice respect, we first need to understand what is going on. Respect is about approaching each other with the same open, objective watchfulness that we use to track the weather. Seeing only what we might want to see—only sunny days, for example—does not give us the information we need to respect the realities at work.

Practicing respect begins, therefore, with seeking to understand what others are thinking and feeling as well as what has happened in their lives, so that we can appreciate why changes are occurring. We each are as we are for reasons, and we change as we do for reasons as well. Practicing respect in an open and unbiased way allows those in our lives to tell us their reasons, their truths, and to walk with us in living them. Giving respect then comes back to us: we find ourselves more able to accept ourselves, to know our own reasons, and to live our truths in a free and open way.

Before a Circle focusing on respect opens, we remind participants that we come together to share stories and learn. Drawing the correlation between respect as a value and the metaphor of a weather gauge, we suggest that respect can serve similarly to help us track the changes going on in ourselves and in those around us. By practicing respect, we can create a safe emotional climate for hearing about the lives of others and perhaps relating their experiences to our own. Respect protects the emotional, mental, physical, social, and spiritual space necessary for us to express ourselves. In a respectful atmosphere, we can address problems and resolve them without assuming that we need to change each other or that one person knows what is best for someone else.

Using a weather gauge as the Circle's centerpiece and a medallion or stone that symbolizes respect as the talking piece, we posed such questions as the following:

- What in your experience fosters disrespect? Consider that this question may have many levels, from personal and family history to social and collective history. How might being aware of these factors affect the level of respect you hold for someone?
- How do you know when you are being respected and when you are not being treated with respect? How do you feel in each case?
- Who in your life have you felt or shown disrespect toward? Would you consider changing this?
- How are you benefited by showing disrespect—what do you gain by doing it? (You must feel a benefit, or you would not do it.) Do you think you could obtain this benefit in another way, a respectful way? How?
- How might you cultivate a respectful approach toward someone for whom you have felt disrespect, especially if you have felt that your disrespect was justified? What role might learning more about the person play? Would a respectful approach involve considering how to address the unresolved issues between you? How might you move toward establishing more respect in this relationship?
- How might finding respectful ways to deal with the problems in your life empower you?

Water

Water is the essence of life, and our bodies are more than half water. We would not think twice about offering a thirsty person or animal a drink of water, and it would be disrespectful to do otherwise. Water cleanses and purifies. Just as our bodies thrive with enough water flowing through us, so, too, do our spirits thrive on the dignity and honor that grows as we give and receive respect. Respect is as life-affirming to our spirits as water is to our bodies.

Using a small fountain or perhaps a bowl of water with a goldfish in it as the centerpiece and a bottle of water as the talking piece, we have framed rounds by inviting participants to consider these questions:

+ How might this bottle of water symbolize aspects of respect as a value?
+ How have you reacted to someone who recently reached out to you for advice, support, or assistance?
+ How do you express respect for yourself and others?
+ What are your relationships like when respect is absent? How might you bring respect into the relationship?

Fire

Fire is powerful. It consumes and changes anyone or anything that comes in contact with it. It does not compromise or negotiate. We use fire for warmth, to cook, to light the way, to celebrate, and to commemorate. Just as fire is constant and unbending, so, too, does respect need to be a constant presence in our lives. When respect is missing from our relationships, the fire that could warm us becomes a fire that consumes us: disrespect fuels anger, resentment, fear, and hatred. Whenever we perpetuate disrespectful relationships, we invite injury or even death, just as if we were walking into a blazing fire. This truth holds collectively as well as personally. Longstanding, collectively endorsed disrespect fuels rage within communities, peoples, and nations, because it consumes the core of our humanity on both sides.

Yet the fire that rages can also be the fire that heals. Fire illuminates where deep healing is needed. In an unlit room at night, the strike of a match can change the mood in an instant. Such is the power of respect. Person to person, extending a respectful hand or offering a respectful distance can transform a negative situation as if by magic. Practicing respect between groups, ethnicities, and nationalities can be as transformative, but it has to be real, courageous, substantive, and consistent to have this positive effect. It has to be fire, not merely smoke.

Using a collage of images of fire as the centerpiece and an empty matchbook as the talking piece, we have raised such questions as the following:

+ What might fire as a metaphor convey to you about respect as a value?
+ Why would you choose to act respectfully?
+ Why would you choose to act disrespectfully?
+ How does respect (or lack of respect) for yourself and others define your relationships?
+ What could you do today that would demonstrate self-respect?
+ What could you do today to respect someone else?

July

The Value of Integrity

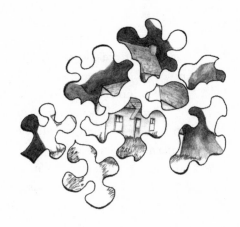

> Integrity is walking with truth and its
> consequences—no matter what.

Integrity speaks to our wholeness. It involves accepting and own-
ing not only those parts of ourselves that we know and show
openly to others but also the parts that we do not see or even
understand. We may not want to confront these parts, we may
find them difficult to deal with, or we may feel shame about them
and want to keep them hidden. Our preference to keep them
"out of sight, out of mind" is, after all, how these parts got tucked
away in the first place.

   Living with integrity means striving to become aware of these
murky, subterranean dimensions inside us. In psychological
terms, the path to integrity takes us straight through our shadow
side: confronting what we least want to look at, addressing the
pain, shame, guilt, unhappiness, helplessness, or fear involved,
and making peace with whatever resides there.

   Integrity calls us to do this not only with ourselves—though
this is certainly the place to begin—but also in our relationships
with others and with situations. More fundamentally, integrity
calls us to do this work within our communities, institutions,
and societies. How did we get to where we are? What lies in our

past or in our present that sits ill with ourselves or others? What harmful patterns do we play a role in perpetuating, intentionally or not? Taking the journey into our shadows is seldom easy, but it is what integrity requires.

Why is embracing our shadow so important? If it is unseen, why can't it stay that way? Integrity is about truth and wholeness. What is unseen is no less real, and its reality affects us just as powerfully as the parts of us that are clearly visible. If we don't know that this side of us exists, it is sure to eventually blindside or sabotage us, because it doesn't go away. Our unseen sides stay with us. When we look at a crescent moon, for example, though we see only a slice of the moon, we know that the whole moon, the total sphere, is orbiting the earth just the same. Or, when we look into a mirror, though we see only the front of our body, we know we have a back side.

So, too, when we are presented with only a portion of a person, relationship, or situation, it would be dishonest and unwise to dismiss the other aspects that make up the whole, the larger reality. A part of a person is not the whole person. One interpretation of a situation is not the whole of what happened. This is why truth heals: truth takes in the whole of who we are and the whole of any experience, and this whole view works things out in a balanced way. Integrity is about embracing the whole precisely when only a part of that whole is presented. Practicing integrity puts us

> "The integrity modeled in the Circle process allows me to share myself with other women. I typically stuff my feelings and thoughts way down inside myself. The Circle has shown me how to open up. It has taught me about the integrity required to make the changes I want to make in my life."
>
> –Circle participant incarcerated at the VOARCC

on the quest to expand our awareness not only of ourselves, each other, relationships, and situations, but also of history and societies. Integrity challenges us to be authentic about the whole of our lives.

Although we already used the process of assembling a jigsaw puzzle as a metaphor for patience, we decided to engage the metaphor of an unassembled jigsaw puzzle again to ponder integrity. Metaphors can be used many ways, and our work in Circles has shown us time and again how many meanings even the simplest metaphors can hold. To illustrate the value of a whole view, it's hard to beat the metaphor of a puzzle.

As puzzle pieces are being laid out, we have no clue how they will all fit together. If we haven't seen the picture on the puzzle box, we don't even know what the completed puzzle will look like. Even if we have seen the picture, the individual pieces bear no resemblance to the overall image. Yet each piece is integral to the puzzle's total design, and throwing out even one piece would diminish the integrity of the final form. Each piece contributes to the puzzle's wholeness and completion, and no piece is unimportant.

What We Used for This Circle

+ An unassembled jigsaw puzzle as the centerpiece
+ A pen for the talking piece

Thoughts for the Circle Opening

We opened the Circle by talking about how living with integrity depends on our powers of self-knowledge and self-inquiry. To know ourselves, we need reliable, appropriate means for externalizing our emotions, thoughts, and experiences—putting them out there, so we can observe them, instead of keeping them buried inside. One way of doing this is to record our inner experiences in a journal. We used a pen as the talking piece to represent this process of self-expression. By expanding our self-knowledge, we build our integrity, which in turn opens us to receive greater knowledge, wisdom, and truth.

Questions for the First Pass

+ How do you become familiar with your thoughts and feelings?
+ What tool might you find helpful for sharing your thoughts and feelings?
+ How does self-revelation and self-awareness relate to your ability to live with integrity?
+ How might a lack of self-awareness cause you to behave in ways that lack integrity?

Questions for the Second Pass

After summarizing what had been shared during the first pass, we posed more questions to invite participants to go deeper into reflecting on the value of integrity:

+ If asked, what would you be willing to share about yourself?
+ What would you want people to say about you?
+ Is the image that you would like to project consistent with your reality as you have come to know yourself?
+ What legacy have you received from your parents and ancestors?
+ What do you think your legacy will be to future generations?
+ What might the issue of multigenerational legacies have to do with integrity?
+ How might awareness of your legacy to future generations affect your choices today?

The Third Pass

Holding the talking piece, we summarized what the participants had shared during the second pass. Before beginning the third pass, we offered each participant a pen and paper and invited her to write down what she wished would happen in her life, what she wanted to accomplish, and how she would like to be remembered. As the participants finished writing, we asked them to put a title on what they had written that would descriptively identify them, such as "Mary the Traveler."

We began the third pass of the talking piece by inviting participants to read what they had written. After each participant had had an opportunity to either read her writing or pass, the talking piece returned to the keeper.

Thoughts for the Circle Closing

To close this Circle, we read a poem that Pat wrote about integrity:

> This life is an ancient flow
> Followed by all
> Walks
> Races
> Religions.
>
> I wade across it,
> Swim against it,
> Lay my boat upon it.
> Flowing with its currents,
> My head held high,
> I enjoy the ride!
> I live with integrity.

We then invited participants to hold their writings and affirm, either out loud or silently:

"This writing reflects my truth and my dreams."

Other Metaphors for Integrity

A House That Needs Repair

We can also compare the job of maintaining personal integrity to that of working on a house that needs fixing. As we move through life, we must continually re-evaluate our lives and, if need be, make some repairs or even do reconstruction.

When a house needs serious reconstruction or remodeling, we have to be careful not to remove any load-bearing walls without first readjusting for the load. Otherwise, the building becomes dangerous and unfit for repair. Similarly, if we don't maintain an accurate assessment of our strengths and vulnerabilities, we risk losing some of our stability and power, like a house that has lost a load-bearing wall.

Home maintenance requires constant attention. Similarly, personal integrity doesn't just happen; it takes continuous work. Integrity needs to be practiced and developed. Over many years and under many circumstances, we learn to accept our strengths and admit our shortcomings. Just as ignoring a leaky roof can cause so much damage that the roof will eventually cave in, so, too, if we persist in denying problems or avoiding issues, it will only be a matter of time before our lives "cave in" on us. The women in prison took this metaphor to heart. One woman said:

> I feel confident that honesty is the best policy and up-
> holds my dignity and integrity. I am encouraged to move
> toward making reparations and amends. The Circle and
> the restorative justice process support my recovery. The
> Circle's involvement is critical in helping me build a foun-
> dation for the changes I am making in my life.

Using pictures of houses in disrepair placed on a base of shredded paper to serve as the centerpiece and a small toy house as the talking piece, we posed some questions:

+ What disrepair do you see in your life that you may not have recognized before?
+ Why were you unable to see the disrepair until now?
+ What room in your home is your favorite room? Why?
+ Where in your home do you feel safest?
+ Has this metaphor brought you any new insights about how to live your life safely and with integrity?

Photographs

A photograph captures a moment in space and time; it allows us to see a slice of life. We take photographs to remind ourselves of times past and times lived well. Often, when someone shows us a photograph, we enjoy the picture, but we also want to hear the story behind it. A photograph invites the viewer to engage the image with curiosity and imagination. So, too, living with integrity invites others to do the same—to share in the commitment to an authentic way of being. The more we strive for integrity in how we live, the more we inhabit who we really are. As with taking photographs, we create memorable impressions of what practicing integrity looks like—what it might mean to live from our wholeness. As we share these images of integrity, we help each other become the kind of people we most want to be.

Several days before the Circle, we invited participants to bring a memorable photograph to the Circle. Using the photographs as the centerpiece and a small, disposable camera (with no working film in it) as the talking piece, we raised some questions:

+ How have you revealed yourself to others?
+ What image do you project to others?
+ Is the picture you project of yourself an honest reflection of who you are and what you feel?
+ How might being truthful, hard as it can be sometimes, help you practice integrity?

- ✦ Can you remember a time when being deceptive or dishonest damaged your sense of your own integrity?
- ✦ What qualities do you respect in others? What conveys integrity to you?

A Personal Journal

In a journal, we record our thoughts, feelings, experiences, and impressions. A journal is a tool of insight and self-revelation, as well as a respected means of communicating with our hearts and minds. Personal journals record our truth and help us understand our authentic selves better. As we learn from our journal writings, we move out into the world with a greater sense of honesty and integrity, because we know more about ourselves.

Using published journals or books of poetry as the centerpiece, and a blank journal book as the talking piece, we asked the following questions:

- ✦ Where or with whom do you express your truth?
- ✦ Would keeping a journal help you live with integrity? How?
- ✦ Why might it be important for you to express your truth in a journal and perhaps even to share some of your self-reflections with someone you trust?
- ✦ How do honesty and self-knowledge enhance your ability to live with integrity?

August

The Value of Courage

> As we walk through our fears, we claim our courage.

When we speak of courage, we generally refer to a quality of mind and spirit that enables us to face difficulty, danger, and pain. Courage challenges us to make changes and face the unknown. With courage, we can move forward without knowing precisely where we are headed and do things that take us far from our comfort zones.

Since exercising courage involves taking risks and acting in spite of uncertainties, the value of courage also calls us to confront our fears. Having courage does not mean we are never afraid; rather, it means we have come to know ourselves and our fears well enough that we can act skillfully and effectively in spite of them. Fears often arise from preconceived thoughts or images of how things will be. Whether our images are accurate or not, our fears signal a need for courage. Integrity helps us practice this value, because it brings our whole being to situations. We are less likely to react from only slices of ourselves, particularly the parts that are afraid.

Yet practicing integrity in itself takes courage. Each day that we strive to act from our wholeness, we must choose to believe in ourselves in spite of doubts, insecurities, and fears. The abandonment we may have experienced from parents, family, friends, or partners can tempt us to abandon ourselves as well. Practicing courage involves resisting this temptation. It calls us to hold fast to a faith and trust in who we are—in our ability to act from what we know and in our commitment to practicing our values. The more we develop self-respect, self-knowledge, and self-acceptance, the more courage we are able to express.

> "When I first came to Circle, I didn't know what to expect. But I discovered myself there, and I became more aware of my feelings. The insights I got from everyone in the Circle helped me be less fearful about what was ahead of me."
>
> –Circle participant incarcerated at the VOARCC

For example, when firefighters enter a burning building, they don't know what they will encounter. They help those in trouble despite unknown dangers and personal risk. They are able to do this because they know what they can and cannot do. They know when to go into the flames and when to leave them.

Drug addicts and alcoholics also exercise courage when they seek recovery. Knowing what their addictions have cost them, they act from a faith that letting go of their old ways will lead to a better life.

In both instances, those challenged to act in these circumstances have no guarantees of success or specific road maps to follow, yet they muster the courage to see the situation through based on what they know about themselves. An action-oriented value, courage gives us the determination to accomplish what may otherwise seem impossible. We gather the strength to face everyday challenges, great and small, and to persist in making positive choices. Practicing courage transforms fear into hope and reveals our true abilities. Practicing courage shows us both who we are and who we can be. One woman talked about the transformation she experienced as a result of her having the courage to attend the Circle:

> "The Circle gave me the emotional support, strength, and courage to do the next right thing."
>
> *–Circle participant incarcerated at the VOARCC*

It took courage for me to be willing to experience this Circle. I didn't know what to expect, but by coming anyway, I discovered more about my behaviors and myself, and I have become more aware of my feelings. By participating in the Circle, I discovered an inner peace that I have not felt in a long time. I now love myself. I am proud of the courage I used to go through this experience, and I am proud of the person I am today.

As our metaphor for courage, we chose a butterfly and its life cycle to symbolize the courage it takes to go through deep changes. The four stages of the butterfly's life—egg, larva (caterpillar), chrysalis, and butterfly—can be compared to stages of development that we also face. Reflecting on the butterfly metaphor, we began to see that when we live life courageously, embracing each phase as it comes, we are able to meet challenges and accomplish our goals.

What We Used for This Circle

+ A centerpiece consisting of a bowl of water, a set of pencils, and "magic paper" strips. (When magic paper

is exposed to water, the paper dissolves. It can be pur-
chased at any art or craft store.)

+ A butterfly image, whether a photo of a butterfly or
a silk or plastic toy butterfly, as the talking piece

Thoughts for the Circle Opening

We opened the Circle by observing that we often need courage
when we are called to act but cannot predict what the outcome
will be. We simply know that an action is necessary, and so we
act in spite of our fears and uncertainties. Whereas integrity expands our self-knowledge and self-awareness, courage puts our
integrity into action. Courage gives us the energy that lifts us out
of fears, calls on our full resources, and connects us with our personal strength and purpose.

Questions for the First Pass

+ How might the metaphor of the stages of a butterfly's
life speak to you about courage? What is it about a
butterfly's life cycle that could inspire courage?
+ What are some of the things that you fear most in
your life?
+ How do you deal with these fears?
+ How does the way that you deal with your fears affect
your response to challenges and hence the outcomes
of your actions?

Questions for the Second Pass

+ Comparing your life to the phases of a butterfly's
growth, which stage do you relate to the most right
now? Which phase might you be experiencing?
+ How might some of the fears you have be associated
with this stage?

+ How might courage help you deal with your current
  challenges?
+ What have you learned from the times that you have
  acted courageously?
+ How might the butterfly metaphor and the value of
  courage help you move through this stage in spite
  of the fears that arise?

The Third Pass

After summarizing what was expressed during the second pass,
we offered the participants magic paper strips and pencils from
the centerpiece and invited them to write one of their fears on
each of the paper strips. We then began the third pass by inviting participants to share the fears they had written down, if they
chose to do so. After each person had had a chance to either
speak or pass, the talking piece returned to the keeper.

Thoughts for the Circle Closing

For our closing, we invited participants to put their magic paper
strips into the bowl of water in the center. As they did, their papers
dissolved and disappeared into the water. We then passed the talking piece once more around the Circle and asked the participants
to share a word that exemplified how they felt at that moment.

Other Metaphors for Courage

Alcoholics Anonymous Medallion

People who choose recovery from addictions take a stand. Yet
this choice is only the first step. Following through requires
courage. It takes courage to consistently seek support, replace
unhealthy choices with healthy ones, and ask for forgiveness.

The members of Alcoholics Anonymous recognize the courage it takes to recover from an addiction by awarding medallions to those who reach certain milestones in recovery. One of the sayings on AA medallions is from Shakespeare's *Hamlet*: "To thine own self be true."

For those recovering from addictions, one of the greatest challenges is to face and endure emotional pain—not to try to escape it. Addictions often stem from a desire to anesthetize painful emotions—to self-medicate away the painful feelings that arise from abuse, trauma, grief, or damaged self-esteem. But in doing so, addictions cut us off from both ourselves and others. Numbing our emotions with addictions, we become less able to respond from our authentic feelings, and we become disconnected from our core being. One woman summarized what being in Circle had taught her about dealing with inner pain:

> My challenge is the blockages between myself and others. In blocking off what hurts me, I wall off my pain. In the long run, blocking off my pain causes more problems for me than the pain itself. If I have the courage to bear my pain instead of blocking it, the pain passes, and I grow from the experience.

Clearly, those who have received medallions for persisting in their recovery have much to teach us. Whether we struggle with an addiction or not, we all occasionally face so much emotional pain that we would rather run away than deal with it. We also find ourselves regularly confronting our powerlessness before some issue and having to exercise courage in order to make healthy, positive changes.

Using an inspirational book as a centerpiece and an Alcoholics Anonymous medallion as the talking piece, we posed several questions:

+ In your experience, have you ever abandoned yourself?
  If so, what did abandoning yourself look like, and how
  did it make you feel?
+ What circumstances or situations might tempt you
  to abandon yourself today?
+ At these times, what might help you to hold firm to
  who you are and what you know?
+ When in your life have you taken a stand for your
  emotional health?
+ What was required of you to take that stand and do
  what was needed?
+ Who in your life has impressed you with a stand he or
  she took and the actions that came with it?
+ What has helped you to act courageously on your own
  behalf or for others?

Rainbows

Rainbows form as storms pass. They create bridges between the
rain and the sun and serve as awesome reminders of the storm's
power to clear the air. To make courageous choices in our lives,
we need to find within our new beginnings the "rainbows" that
reassure us we are moving out of stormy times and into new ways
of living. Our personal rainbows may take the form of supportive
people, goals we have achieved, or concrete changes in our lives as
we move from storm to peace.

Using pictures of storms and rainbows as the centerpiece and
a crystal to symbolize the rainbow's reflection of light as the talking piece, we framed several rounds with some questions:

+ What personal storms have you recently been through?
+ Were you able to exercise courage in how you dealt with
  your storm?
+ Did you experience any rainbows as the storm passed?

+ How did you recognize these rainbows? Did they encourage you to continue making courageous choices?

Bridges

Bridges connect. They enable us to cross from one point to another and so, metaphorically, remind us of the courage it takes to
make that crossing. Bridges support travelers by helping us reach
otherwise inaccessible destinations. Just as a bridge connects one
point to another, so, too, courage helps us reach across the unknown or seemingly impossible chasms and arrive on the other
side. To take this journey, we often depend on others to help us
make changes and alter unhealthy emotional and behavioral patterns. Reaching out and building bridges takes courage and commitment, but if we build our bridges on as much solid ground as
possible, we can go forward in creating lives that would be hard if
not impossible to create without these supports.

Using a model bridge as the centerpiece and a paper chain as
the talking piece, we posed these questions:

+ What connections do you need to make so that you
  will be supported in changing your life?
+ Will it take courage for you to make these connections?
+ Why is it important to build your personal bridges
  on solid ground? What might this mean, practically
  speaking?

Autumn

Autumn's exhale shows me a new face.
Each day another family of birds takes flight from their
summer home.
Searching for a forgotten blueberry patch,
Black bears prepare to settle in.
Low-lying vines and sumac put on their red clothes,
While bees and ants stock up in a frenzy.

I give thanks to the spirit of autumn.
I welcome the spirit of autumn.

—Excerpt from a poem by Susan Thompson

September

The Value of Generosity

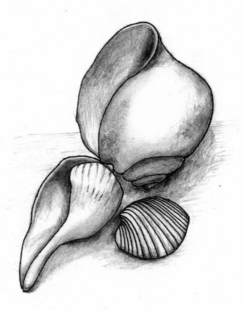

The ring of giving and receiving
Has nothing to do with the ring of
Work
Compensation
Possessions
Assets
Purchases.
It is a ring of true giving
With no strings,
From the heart.

To have expectations
Is to keep the intention of giving
From traveling full circle.

To share the magic of the ring
Is to give a gift truly
And then to let it go.

Pay attention
Be alert!
You'll know the gift made full circle
When you see wonderful things happening:
Doors open,
Love ignites,
Friendships are born,
Prosperity grows,
And forgiveness spreads its balm.

· Susan Thompson

Autumn, a time when the natural world releases its bounty, offers powerful images of generosity. Trees, flowers, and plants yield fruit, nuts, and vegetables in abundance during the harvest, and this abundance sustains life during the year to come. Yet the harvest does not happen in a vacuum. To yield its abundance, the natural world must receive energy from the sun, water from the snow and rain, and nutrients from the earth. Nature's cycle of giving and receiving generates growth, and we are part of this cycle.

Observing this two-way flow, we learn the art of giving and receiving, which we need to participate in to survive. The dominant view is that our survival demands that we only take, but this view is not consistent with what happens in the natural world. Giving is as essential to our survival as receiving. These two components create a flow that we experience as generosity, and it makes our world abundant. Giving and receiving smooth and equalize. They move energies around to maintain a healthy, sustainable, thriving balance. They also generate understanding, compassion, gratitude, and community. In our September Circles, we explore how the twofold rhythm of generosity reflects the natural pulse of life and why engaging in this flow is critical to our well-being and continued survival.

What We Used for This Circle

+ A centerpiece of a wooden bowl of acorns
+ An oak leaf for the talking piece

Thoughts for the Circle Opening

Sue's experience of attending the feast at the Women of Nations Eagle's Nest Shelter, described earlier in this book, was a turning point in her life. In particular, it deepened her sense of generosity, since the women's shelter organized the feast to thank the community for its support. Pondering this experience, she later wrote:

> The afternoon was both a celebration of gratitude and an act of generosity. Before the day ended, we all shared the meal, and everyone left with a gift.
>
> At home, my daughter and I reflected on the amazing afternoon we experienced. I told my daughter that the women hosting the event were truly women of generosity. They were giving back to the community in order to thank the community for the care and love it had extended to them. It gave me a chance to talk to my daughter about the power of receiving and the generosity of giving—that it is just as generous to receive as it is to give. By accepting another's gift, we give that person the opportunity to experience the gift called generosity. This experience remains pivotal for both my daughter and me in appreciating the value of generosity and how it works.

To illustrate the two-way flow of taking in and giving out, we asked the Circle participants to notice for a moment the two-way "giving" and "receiving" of their breathing and to focus on the acorn centerpiece. Each tiny acorn holds the potential to become a huge oak tree, and every year each oak tree generates hundreds of acorns. From a single acorn, then, thousands upon thousands of acorns can be created over time. In our Circles, the tiny acorns have served as metaphors for a generosity that is not just abundant but superabundant. The acorn metaphor also shows that generosity and abundance are the ways of the natural world.

Questions for the First Pass

We wanted to start by bringing the value of generosity home to the participants' everyday lives, so we framed the first round with a few basic questions:

+ Why is receiving a generous act?
+ What type of support do you need, and how do you go about getting your needs met?
+ How might the two-way flow of giving and receiving help you meet your needs?
+ What type of support and nurturance might you offer to someone in your life?
+ How do you feel when you act generously to someone?

Questions for the Second Pass

For the second round, we asked participants to reflect on the flow of giving and receiving:

+ What "fruits" or gifts flow from your nature and essence, from who you are?
+ Which is easier for you: giving or receiving?
+ What might you need to receive to express your gifts more fully?
+ What might make it easier for you to share your gifts with others?
+ What might help you become more comfortable with receiving gifts from others?

Questions for the Third Pass

Before beginning the third pass, we invited each participant to take an acorn from the centerpiece, and then we posed the following questions:

+ What does this acorn symbolize for you?
+ What will you do with this acorn?
+ What does the value of generosity mean to you?
+ When you participate in both giving and receiving, how does this affect your sense of being in the world? How might life seem to you when giving and receiving flow in a balanced way?

Thoughts for the Circle Closing

To close the Circle, we read a poem that Pat wrote:

> Give thanks to the sky
>   to the stars
>   to the moon
>   to the sun.
> Give thanks to the winds
>   to the rains
>   to the storms.
> Give thanks to the earth
>   to the streams
>   to the mountains
>   the animals
>   the flowers and birds.
> Give thanks
>   for receiving
>   for connecting
>   for being.

More Metaphors for Generosity

Elders

Many of our elders—family members, colleagues, friends, and community members—exemplify humility and generosity. They have come to appreciate the gift of life, and they understand its fragility. Over the course of their lives, they have seen how often life teeters between good times and rough times. Through years of experiences, they have gained a profound knowledge of the cycles of life—a perspective that only time and experience can give. If we want to learn how to start from where we are standing, our wise ones can show us how. Elders often hold treasures that are available to us for the asking. They exemplify generosity, because they have arrived at their elderhood by living in the continual two-way flow of giving and receiving. Not otherwise could they have survived their many years on any level of their lives—physical, mental, emotional, or spiritual.

Using a collage of pictures or photographs of elders as the centerpiece and a heart touchstone as the talking piece, we posed some questions to invite thought and reflection:

- What have been some of your experiences with people whom you might consider to be an "elder" in your life?
- In what ways might the elders in your life model the art of giving and receiving?
- How might the elders in your life exemplify the value of generosity?
- What might you learn from elders that could enhance your practice of generosity?

Shells

Sea creatures build their shells over the course of their lives. When the creatures die, their shells continue to exist, potentially for thousands of years. Limestone is created when the earth's gravity compacts billions of shells over eons. The creatures draw minerals from the sea, which they exude from their bodies to form shells that grow with them. When they die, their shells return the gift of the minerals they have taken by creating stunning mountains and cliffs, which provide essential nutrients for other life forms. Just as shells are shed through the natural life cycle, so, too, can we generously offer our assets to assist or support others. By engaging in receiving and returning, we contribute to the flow that sustains life.

When we hold a single shell, we are reminded of the life that once created it. Once shed, shells are left for us to find and admire, to keep as pieces of art, or to reflect on as touchstones. Shells remind us to move with life's flow, to accept life in its comings and goings, and to share with others the gifts we have received.

Using a bowl of seashells as the centerpiece and a single, larger shell as the talking piece, we have initiated rounds by asking the following questions:

+ What gift have you recently given to someone?
+ What gift have you recently accepted?
+ How did you feel when you were giving or receiving a gift?

Smiles

What is more wonderful than to receive a smile? Smiling is a natural act of generosity. It is rare that we don't feel happier when someone smiles at us. Moreover, a smile invariably makes not only the receiver but also the giver feel better, for seldom do we give a smile that we do not receive something in return. This exchange of giving and receiving is inherent in a smile, making smiles an ideal metaphor for generosity and its two-way flow.

Using photographs of people smiling as the centerpiece and a smiling-face sticker as the talking piece, we posed some questions:

+ When did someone recently offer you a smile, and what were the circumstances?
+ How did you feel when that person smiled at you?
+ In what situation recently did you offer someone else a smile?
+ How did you feel after smiling at the person?

October

The Value of Forgiveness

Burdened with anger,
my heart closes, and
my journey halts.
Forgiveness opens my heart,
and my journey begins again.

In October, the signs of autumn are everywhere. Daylight shortens. Turtles and frogs disappear into mud banks or under leaves. Lush, green foliage turns to gold, red, and orange. Fruits, nuts, and vegetables drop from trees and vines, while leaves fall from their branches. Robins, loons, herons, egrets, and hummingbirds take off from their summer homes and fly south. October's autumn provides many images of letting go, and these images from the seasonal cycle teach us that letting go is a natural and necessary response to life's changes.

What do we let go of? Using the metaphor of these natural processes, we let go of things that have fulfilled their purpose in our life's cycle. Holding on to them longer would not be healthy. Anger provides a good example. Anger is important for us to maintain healthy boundaries. When we suffer injustice, for instance, we should be angry; self-respect and self-esteem require it. We deserve to be treated fairly and with respect, and anger warns us that this may not be happening. The same with pain and hurt: these natural feelings protect us. The pain of burning our hand if we get too close to a fire gives us information we need about both the power of fire and our body's boundaries. The pain of a relationship in deep change tells us that we have issues that we must address.

Whatever messages anger, frustration, grief, or pain may carry, they always tell us something about our lives. They may, for example, tell us that things are going down a dangerous road or that our expectations and desires may not fit certain realities. They may also tell us that we have suffered hurt but are not yet ready to deal with it.

Because our emotions come to us for reasons that have to do with who we are and where we are in our development, they warrant our respect and serious, open, and unprejudiced attention. Why are we feeling this way? Where is this emotion coming from? Are we getting its message? And what are we doing about it? In a sense, emotions are the fruits of our life choices and experiences. If we accept them as such, they nourish our growth. To use the seasonal metaphor, we "harvest" the messages behind our emotions and turn them into positive self-awareness and constructive actions. When our emotions have done their job of sending us warnings and other calls to awareness and action, we let them go as a natural response.

The trouble arises when, for whatever reason, we don't receive our emotions' messages or don't know what to do with them. If we deny our emotions, they persist unprocessed, undigested. That is when they become unhealthy, even toxic. Stuck in an emotional bind, we hang on to a particular feeling. If we don't let it go, it builds, presumably because its message has not yet been received or the issues behind it are not being addressed. Its volume increases. Holding on to emotions—especially the more intense, difficult, and painful ones—signals that something is unbalanced or outright blocked. We feel at odds with our natural rhythm, whose momentum keeps urging us forward.

Hanging on to difficult emotions is clearly dangerous. We are the ones at greatest risk of being hurt, although conflicted and un-resolved emotions take an equally heavy toll on our relationships. Stuck emotions eat away at us. They can make us physically sick, or they can prompt us to turn to alcohol, drugs, or other addictions to temporarily alleviate the resulting torment. Stuck anger and resentment drain our energies and can prevent us from taking positive steps toward rectifying whatever is out of balance.

To use the metaphor of autumn, if migrating birds failed to fly south, they would most likely not survive the winter. Fruits and vegetables would rot if they stayed on the vine. So, too, anger bottled up for long periods hardens into resentment or hate, and pain and hurt settle into our psyches as festering wounds. Even emotions we enjoy can go sour if we hang on to them too long. They can become inauthentic masks—facades of cheeriness—that don't allow us to track the realities we face or the changes we're undergoing.

How can we get unstuck? In other words, how can we channel the energies of our emotions in ways that make us wiser and stronger—more mindful of ourselves and more able to act appropriately given the dynamics at work in our lives? This is where the value of forgiveness comes in.

Forgiveness is a controversial value, in part because of the inappropriate expectations that often shroud it. Victims of harm often feel pressured to forgive those who harmed them before they are inwardly ready to do so and before outward acts of rectification and justice have been made. Some universities now have a field called "Forgiveness Studies," because the process is so complex yet also so essential to personal, family, social, and emotional health. Maybe someday there will also be "Humility Studies," "Patience Studies," or "Respect Studies," but for now, the value of forgiveness is both sufficiently needed and sufficiently difficult to warrant a discipline of its own.

From the seasonal metaphor, though, we find some important clues about how forgiveness might work. Forgiveness seems to start with honoring the meaning or reasons behind our emotions—why we have them. We "harvest" our emotions by appreciating their significance in our lives. This awareness may also lead to various forms of action. Perhaps we need to establish more healthy boundaries; maybe we need to address a conflict that we've been avoiding; perhaps we need to work through some lingering pain, fear, or trauma; or maybe we need to take some outward action to defend ourselves and seek justice. After we deal with the emotion's message and its practical implications—however we choose to do this—we can then release the emotion, since its job is done. Like the letting go that happens in the natural world during autumn, we release our emotions naturally; the process doesn't have to be forced.

> "The Circle showed me that it is okay to have and express my feelings. It has helped me change by being able to release my issues and my pain. I am grateful for the opportunity to release my anger, stress, and pain."
>
> —Circle participant incarcerated at the VOARCC

Framing forgiveness this way, we can practice this value for our emotional health and well-being, so that we can stay in sync with our own natural cycles. Forgiveness in this sense is not about determining whether or not another person is worthy or deserving of forgiveness. Neither is forgiveness something to be withheld as a way to punish whoever harmed us. The process is fundamentally about us: what we need to do in order to be healthy and to go forward with our lives.

Forgiveness—accepting our emotions, learning from them, and then releasing them—becomes a way of life, because it enables us to stay in tune with our growth cycles and not get stuck at any one stage.

All beings in nature move instinctively with the natural cycle from summer to fall to winter back to spring. By surrendering to this cycle and its wisdom, we live on. Patterning the releasing of autumn, forgiveness challenges us to move through our emotions—especially the ones we are most prone to get stuck in—so that we can arrive at another place in our hearts and minds. By doing so, we choose to go on living in wiser, more open, and ultimately more effective ways.

What We Used for This Circle

+ A centerpiece consisting of pictures that express the feeling of autumn, placed on a blanket of dried leaves
+ A chain of keys for the talking piece

Thoughts for the Circle Opening

Calling attention to the chain of keys, we talked about the chains of relationships, circumstances, and events in our lives. Between each link in the chain are spaces where more keys can be added. So, too, our lives are linked by spaces that give us room in which to move, change, alter our circumstances, and re-form our relationships. In these spaces between our connections, letting go—the key to forgiveness—can occur.

Before passing the talking piece, we read some short pieces that we wrote around the themes of autumn and forgiveness:

Forgiveness nurtures our spirits with freedom and new possibilities. It releases anger, guilt, resentment, and revenge and brushes our spirits with calm and peace.

How do I let go?
I have learned to acquire,
But how do I learn to let go?

Maybe now is the time.
Will learning this make life easier?
Will the lesson bring answers
Or more questions?
Can I let go?

Autumn
Trees let go of leaves.
The day lets go of light.

I see the empty nest,
The one that took days to build
With wings and beak,
The one that held three eggs.

The trees
The day
The nest
The bird

All let go
To wind
To rain
To cold.

Questions for the First Pass

Before passing the talking piece, we spoke about forgiveness as an ongoing process and as something we do for ourselves. Practicing forgiveness daily fosters self-love, because it calls us to spend time with our feelings and to respect why they exist. Our emotions are worth being taken seriously; they don't arise for no reason. We also accept ourselves when we allow ourselves to change and to move past this or that feeling.

As we accept ourselves more, we find that we are able to accept others as they are too, and this eases our relationships. Our inner experience of the world shifts from a place of defensiveness, conflict, and hurt to a place where nurturing and assurance reside. To engage participants in contemplating forgiveness as a value, we framed the first round with some basic questions:

+ What might the season of autumn convey to you about forgiveness?
+ What place does forgiveness have in your life?
+ Can you recall a situation where you practiced forgiveness? What inner process did this involve for you? How did you do it?
+ How did practicing forgiveness in that situation affect your emotions?
+ How have you felt when you were able to release painful emotions that you had been holding toward someone?
+ Is there someone on your chain of life who may be holding hard feelings toward you? How might your commitment to practicing forgiveness cause a shift in your relationship?
+ How do you feel when others release negative emotions they have held toward you?

Questions for the Second Pass

After summarizing the first pass, we discussed how the forgiveness process begins with opening up about past hurts or harms. Very often, current harms bring to the surface unresolved pain around older hurts, even going back to childhood. Indeed, our intense feelings may be more about what happened in the past than about the current situation. Realizing this—and how past events may be affecting our emotions about a current situation—helps us identify and then release painful feelings from both the past and the present. Along these lines, we invited participants to consider these questions:

+ What might you do to begin the forgiveness process around some situation in your life? Where might you start?

+ What feelings might you need to acknowledge and deal with during the forgiveness process?

+ Are some of your feelings carried over from past experiences? How much of your emotional intensity has to do with what you have experienced in the past, and how much comes from what is going on now?

+ What key might help you unlock a door that is blocking you from engaging your emotions and releasing them? How can you "harvest" the messages embedded in your feelings about a person, situation, or event—then and now—so that you can then let these feelings go?

Questions for the Third Pass

After summarizing the second pass, we suggested that forgiveness also involves examining the situation as openly and objectively as possible. How might things appear from different points of view? Emotions provide one level of information about painful experiences, but other levels of information might be important to consider as well. Before inviting the participants to reflect on the process of forgiveness further, we suggested that each participant remove a key from the chain when the key-chain talking piece was handed to her:

+ Do you currently feel stuck in your emotions around some person, circumstance, or event that practicing forgiveness might ease?

+ What key might help you open the door to letting go, so that your emotions could flow more easily?

+ What other points of view might shed light on the experience?
+ If practicing forgiveness is how you want to deal with this experience, what has helped you to become ready to do this?
+ Do you feel that an apology might be appropriate for whatever role you might have had in the situation? If so, how might you apologize? Might additional actions be needed in order to create a good balance between you?
+ Have you considered practicing forgiveness toward yourself? Is there something you have done that you might want to forgive yourself for doing? How might you go about forgiving yourself? Where would you start?

Thoughts for the Circle Closing

Holding the keys we personally took from the key-chain talking piece when it was our turn to speak, we said to participants:

> Keep this key to remind you that you hold the key to unlocking every possibility for forgiveness and healing in your life. As you release anger, resentment, rejection, and revenge, you forgive and heal, and your heart becomes lighter and stronger. You hold the key. See what it opens.

Other Metaphors for Forgiveness

A Bottle of Sparkling Water

If we shake a bottle of sparkling water, we stir up the carbonation inside. If we keep shaking the bottle and then open it, the water sprays in every direction to release the pressure. Similarly, if we hold feelings of anger or resentment inside and don't pay attention to their messages enough to release them, we want to explode. Even though we may know intellectually that we need to move on, as long as we avoid dealing with the issues and our intense feelings around them, our emotional pressure will mount. If this pressure builds up long enough, we'll experience some form of emotional crisis.

To prevent an explosion of fizzy drink, we open the bottle slowly and carefully. Likewise, to avoid emotional meltdowns, we learn to process our emotions appropriately as they arise and then release them. We try not to let upset feelings back up on us. Granted, it takes time and practice to let go of people or situations that have caused us pain. Forgiveness is a journey; it does not happen overnight. As with the other values, practicing forgiveness is a way of life. Being willing to forgive—and understanding how to do it—releases feelings through a healthy, respectful process and helps us avoid emotional buildup. It clears the way for us to be the people we want to be, so that we can move forward in our lives.

Using a carton of individual plastic bottles of sparkling water as the centerpiece and a single plastic bottle of sparkling water as the talking piece, we posed a few questions:

- What feelings or fears might be bottled up inside you?
- What is it like when you hold feelings inside that you wish you could find a way to express or resolve?
- Why do you hold on to your feelings? What prevents you from working through them and letting them go? How can identifying these obstacles help you access your natural ability to process your emotions?
- What might your first steps be in slowly and carefully releasing your pent-up feelings?
- How might practicing forgiveness help you release emotions that you may have been carrying for a long time?

A Handful of Sand

Have you ever tried to hold a handful of sand? Sand naturally slips through your fingers. Like sand, our feelings naturally flow through us. Yet this natural process is often blocked when we feel difficult or painful emotions—emotions that are not easy to share. Granted, painful feelings are hard to process, and their messages can seem unpleasant and unwelcome. We may not want to hear what our emotions are telling us, or we may not know what to do with the messages even when we get them. Facing what feels like an emotional impasse, we let feelings sit and fester, instead of expressing them appropriately and letting them "flow through."

Using a bowl of sand as the centerpiece and a vial of sand as the talking piece, we invited participants to consider a few questions:

- What feelings are sitting in you that may need attention, expression, and release—the practice of forgiveness?
- What is the nature of a resentment you may be carrying?
- How might forgiveness help you to release it?
- Who is it that most needs to be forgiven? In other words, toward whom do you direct negative feelings and judgments most often?
- What might help you to release these stuck feelings, so that they can flow through you?

Windows

Closed windows with the drapes pulled or blinds drawn shut out the light. Inside the room, our experience is limited. The room may feel safe and comfortable at first, but over time it feels restrictive and unhealthy. We may even feel trapped. Opening the windows changes the atmosphere immediately, bringing in a breath of fresh air along with a view of what's outside. Whereas covered windows narrow us to what's inside, open windows con-nect us with the great outdoors.

Much like living behind closed windows, holding on to anger, resentment, or fear causes these feelings to overshadow our ex-periences. Over time, our spirit grows heavy, and an unhealthy emotional environment sets in. The way to break through this closed state is to open our hearts to understanding and forgive-ness, which naturally lightens the atmosphere. No longer trapped inside negative emotions, we feel released and open ourselves to wider possibilities.

Using a collage of windows that are open and closed, draped and undraped, as the centerpiece and a picture of the sun to sym-bolize the expansive energy of forgiveness as the talking piece, we posed some questions:

+ In what ways might you be closing yourself off to people, places, and things?
+ Why might you be inclined to do this?
+ How does it feel when your inner space feels narrowed, limited, and closed off? Are there times when you need this? Why? How might this closed-off atmosphere not be a help to you?
+ How might practicing forgiveness make it easier for you to relax and open up?
+ Can you think of anything that might be preventing you from releasing your feelings and offering forgiveness to someone in your life?

November

The Value of Gratitude

Manifested in smiles,
words of encouragement,
or sounds of joy and
pleasure, gratitude creates
positive spaces in our lives.

By November, the abundant growth that has occurred since spring has been harvested, so that we can now appreciate the good that the seasonal changes have brought. November tends to be a time of going inward and reflecting. Even the mice move indoors, while other critters grow thick coats and burrow in for the winter. The air chills, the light fades, and a hush falls, punctuated by the occasional sound of a whirling wind. The smell of wood smoke is in the air. As nature moves toward a period of dormancy, we embrace the subdued November palette. The harvest celebrations of many Indigenous cultures give thanks for the abundance of months past and express gratitude for how that abundance will now support life during the leaner months to come.

November can therefore be an appropriate time to reflect on the value of gratitude, which is a simpler and more straightforward value than October's forgiveness. No matter what the circumstances, we can almost always find something to be grateful for. It is a natural and easy response. As soon as we reflect on the good around us and appreciate the opportunities that have come our way, we feel grateful, no matter how demanding the journey may have been. Gratitude opens our hearts to new possibilities. As years pass, we realize that difficult or painful times have also led to unimagined blessings.

Gratitude helps us notice this. It inspires a wider perspective and helps us cope with life's ups and downs with more balance. As with the other values, living from a sense of gratitude is a conscious choice—one that we make day by day, until it becomes a way of life. Perhaps more than any other value, though, gratitude provides a potent antidote to sadness, loneliness, fear, and negative thoughts. Gratitude cuts through heaviness and lifts us up.

What We Used for This Circle

+ A clock for the centerpiece
+ A wristwatch for the talking piece to symbolize the passage of time
+ Closing gifts of note cards and stamped envelopes

Thoughts for the Circle Opening

Being present in the moment and appreciating who and what is present with us are skills we can cultivate. Since grief, worries, and expectations often make us lose sight of the good in our lives, pausing to appreciate things—as if this were our last moment on earth—brings us back to what is important. A more reflective view inspires us to be grateful in simple, humble, and strengthening ways. By engaging in the art of appreciative noticing one moment at a time, we develop an abiding sense of gratitude. The two of us have written some poems on the value of gratitude, which we often read to open a Circle on this value:

Gratitude creates room in our hearts,
The rainbow across a stormy sky
That lets in unexpected beauty.

Gratitude carries a message of hope,
The blessing of a warm welcome.

Gratitude comforts our hearts,
Eliminates fear,
Embraces our efforts,
One moment at a time.

Questions for the First Pass

+ What might the metaphor of November's harvest suggest to you about gratitude as a value?
+ What do you value most in your life? What in your life do you feel good about? What do you appreciate?
+ In what ways might gratitude be an important value for you to cultivate? How might it help you?
+ How might you cultivate gratitude in spite of limited or painful circumstances?
+ How might cultivating a sense of gratitude enhance your self-esteem and relationships?

Questions for the Second Pass

+ Who has recently helped you in some way?
+ What did this person do for you?
+ How did his or her support make you feel about yourself or your life?
+ Have you been able to express your gratitude to this person?

Questions for the Third Pass

Following the summary of the second pass, we offered a note card to each participant and invited her to write the name of a person who had helped her recently. We then posed another set of questions for participants to consider:

+ Whose name did you write on your card?
+ If you sent a "Thank You" card to this person, what would you write in it?

Thoughts for the Circle Closing

With these note cards as closing gifts to the participants, we passed out stamped envelopes for the cards and suggested that participants consider writing to the people who had been helpful to them. By expressing their gratitude to these individuals, they would be creating spaces for those who received the cards to feel gratitude in return—gratitude for the opportunity to have become part of their lives in some meaningful, memorable way.

More Metaphors for Gratitude

Honey

Honey sweetens a slice of bread, improves the taste of a vinegar dressing, and transforms bitter tea into a sweet, refreshing drink. Like honey, gratitude brings sweetness to our lives. Being grateful can turn a difficult situation around and open us to solutions that we simply could not see or perhaps even imagine before. One grateful thought can lift the weight of hardship or grief. Practicing gratitude is a choice, and one that has the power to transform us. Fear, unhappiness, self-doubt, and a gnawing criticism of others give way to a sense of generosity and of being at peace with things.

Using a honey-sweetened dessert as the centerpiece and a bottle of honey as the talking piece, we posed some questions:

+ Where in your life might a sense of gratitude ease concerns, lighten things up, and possibly even transform a situation?
+ Why would you choose gratitude as a good response in this situation?
+ When you go through a difficult time in your life, how might it help you to find something to be grateful for? If gratitude does bring sweetness, how and why might it do this? What are the dynamics here?
+ How might a sense of gratitude help you connect with supportive people?

A Cornucopia or Horn of Plenty

A horn of plenty, overflowing with fruits, nuts, and vegetables, represents the abundance of life's harvest. It suggests that, if we live in balance with the natural world, our needs will be met in a free and full way. The image inspires gratitude—an ability to appreciate what has come to us as well as an ability to let go of feeling driven by wants or insatiable desires. It also signifies an awareness that, although we may not always get what we want in life, we will most likely get what we need.

Using a cornucopia as the centerpiece and a piece of fruit as the talking piece, we framed the rounds with some questions:

+ Imagine your life as a horn of plenty: what lies inside that horn for you?
+ What do you need, and how might that be different from what you want?

+ What in your life do you feel most grateful for?
+ How do you express gratitude for what is in your life today?

Rope

A rope secures, lifts, and protects. When we need a rope, we're grateful to have one, and we're desperate if we don't. A rope can be a lifeline that pulls us out of danger. Similarly, gratitude can pull us out of hopelessness, depression, anger, or fear. Sometimes we just need to grab hold of gratitude in spite of everything and hang on to it like a lifeline. If we choose to practice gratitude diligently, the gratitude that takes hold of us has the power to lift us out of self-pity, loneliness, and despair. It ties us to what is good in our lives, and this can pull us through.

A rope can also provide a good metaphor for considering how we can go about meeting our needs in contrast to pursuing our desires. Every desire we pursue can represent another knot we tie in the rope. The more wants we have, the more knotted the rope becomes. It gets shorter and shorter, until it is a tight ball. Gratitude suggests that we could use the rope differently. We appreciate that the rope holds us and that it is most flexible and effective when it has the least number of knots in it. Gratitude for the good already present in our lives unties unnecessary knots, and this open appreciation makes us more receptive to how the rope can support us.

Using an object that is secured by a rope as the centerpiece and a piece of rope tied with different knots as the talking piece, we invited participants to reflect on this metaphor and its many meanings for our emotional journeys:

+ What situation in your life makes you feel tied up in knots?

+ How did you get into the situation? Who or what tied these knots?
+ How might you change the situation?
+ What role might gratitude have in unraveling the tightness?
+ How might practicing gratitude as a way of life provide a lifeline for you?

Winter

To stand all winter, bare branches in frigid winds:
This is a mystery to me.
This is a gift to me.

I stand at an end and at a beginning.
Teach me to bear the cold.
Give me strength to go through the snow.
Show me the beauty in the barren landscape.
Give me dreams to carry me through.
Tell me stories to keep me warm.

· *Excerpt from a poem by Susan Thompson*

December

The Value of Wisdom

Wisdom is being
at peace with
our truth.

From autumn, the cycle of the seasons shifts to winter. We no longer hear insects humming or bees buzzing. Many of the song-birds have gone quiet, and in their place, crows, woodpeckers, geese, hawks, and eagles can now be heard. Daylight fades, and night lengthens. As we pile on heavy clothes, we join nature in withdrawing to rest, so we can reflect and dream. Winter presents yet a different face of change—sometimes subtle, sometimes harsh. It is not within our power to say "yes" or "no" to the natural passage of time, but from that inexorable passage, we develop wisdom. As we pass through cycle after cycle, our awareness deepens about who we are and our sense of meaning and purpose in life. Over the many winters of our lives, wisdom takes root in us.

During winter, the natural world pares down to its essence: trees become bare, and only seeds and bulbs remain from lush summer plants. It is a demanding, testing time as well: cold, wind, snow, little light, not much food, frozen water. Winter provides a metaphor for contemplating how we face our "winters": How do we prepare for the hard and lean times? Where do we find light during the long nights created by loss and disillusionment, grief or despair? How can we share our experiences of pain and vulnerability or open our hearts to each other when so much has happened that could make us feel cold and isolated?

Wisdom as a value can speak to these questions, but wisdom does not emerge all at once. It develops as we practice all the other values over years. Bringing our best values to countless experiences, we become wiser about the role that values play in our lives, and we come to trust their power to help us work things out in good ways. The more we let our best values guide our response to difficult or painful situations, the more we learn how to transform experiences, so they lead to positive results. This knowledge is the essence of wisdom, distilled from a lifetime of experiences.

> "What I like most about the Circle is its sacredness. The Circle gives me a chance to release a part of myself and to share a piece of who I am with other women. I learn more about myself and am stirred to approach the obstacles in my life differently."
>
> –Circle participant incarcerated at the VOARCC

Indeed, it takes a lifetime to grow wise, and even then, not everyone chooses a road that leads there. Some of the most profound lessons come through pain and suffering. As years pass, we may well have been burned many times. We may be tempted to emerge from the flames with bitterness, cynicism, and a steely resolve to harden our defenses, so that we don't get burned again. Though wisdom helps us distinguish what is wise from what is foolish, wisdom is not about building walls or defenses—distancing ourselves from the passion and vulnerability of life. Things that are hard break easily, and defenses shut out more than they let in. Wisdom shows us how to stay soft and flexible precisely when our inclination would be to withdraw and become tough and defensive. Wisdom gives us the courage to keep our hearts open and courageously vulnerable, for otherwise we cannot generate the warmth—the deep human intimacy—that we need to stay alive.

The wisdom we gain can be expressed in many ways. Above all, it is expressed in how we respond to people and situations. We each have our own ways of passing on our wisdom. One way that is common worldwide is storytelling: sharing within a community the journeys others have taken, the decisions they made, and the consequences that followed. Conveying wisdom through storytelling provides a strong link to the winter season, which is the traditional time for this activity. The long winter nights with their quiet, contemplative tone create an ideal space for sharing stories. Weaving entertainment with teaching, stories pass on the wisdom of generations, so that the roads we choose can eventually lead to a wisdom that becomes our own.

What We Used for This Circle

+ A large candle for the centerpiece
+ A paper star for the talking piece
+ Closing gifts of holiday cards and stamped envelopes

> "The Circle made me become more aware of myself and enabled me to speak in front of others. The stories everyone shared with me were enlightening."
>
> *–Circle participant incarcerated at the VOARCC*

Thoughts for the Circle Opening

During long, crisp, winter nights, we have time to see the stars. We seem to appreciate them more, because the dark winter sky makes them stand out. Scientists might scan the sky for decades before they discover a new star. When a star is finally discovered, it comes into our collective consciousness from a place of obscurity.

To apply the metaphor, wisdom comes to us through many years of living our truth as best we can and engaging our values as stars to guide us. The wisdom we gain can then help light the paths of others. By sharing our experiences, we exchange notes about how to live our values—how to use values to channel our thoughts and energies in good ways.

With a large candle as the centerpiece and a paper star as the talking piece, we told the participants that we were going to turn out the lights for a short time and light the candle. We then read some thoughts we wrote about wisdom:

> *Wisdom grows as we learn to live in peace with our mistakes. Taken to heart, our mistakes increase our knowledge of life and deepen our compassion for ourselves and others: this is the way of the wise.*

We turned the lights back on and left the candle burning.

Questions for the First Pass

We commented that we each have had experiences that could make us wiser if we brought the lessons from these experiences to consciousness. But to benefit from the wisdom embedded in these experiences, we need to coax our memories of them out from under the heavy mantle of fear, denial, or shame and into the open atmosphere of acceptance and truth. We invited participants to consider their own experiences:

- What memorable experience comes to mind as you sit watching this candle?
- Why is this experience memorable for you?
- How long has it been since you thought of this experience?

+ What wisdom might this experience bring into
your life?
+ How might the wisdom you gained from this experience help you in the future?

Questions for the Second Pass

Making sense of events takes time, since our inner processing of experiences happens at its own pace. We need to digest
experiences, talk about them, and listen to what others have
to say. Through this activity, we build a sense of meaning and
purpose—why certain things happened, what good may have
come from them, and the wisdom these experiences might bring
to us. Though this process does not happen overnight, with time
our hearts generally come to terms with whatever we have experienced. To frame a second round, we posed another set of
questions:

+ What life experience would you like to learn more from
and perhaps gain a greater sense of inner peace about?
+ Why did you choose this experience?
+ How have you thought about this experience in the
past? What feelings come up for you as you remember
it? For example, does thinking about this experience
make you feel bitter, resentful, or angry?
+ If you have thought about this experience before, have
you been tempted to become cynical or pessimistic?
+ What is the difference between wisdom and cynicism
or pessimism? What would make you go to one place
or the other—wisdom or cynicism? What role might
practicing the other values have in deciding the direction you end up going?
+ How might practicing the other values help you gain

wisdom from this experience? Which values in particular might be helpful?
+ How might the wisdom you have gained from other
experiences help you to process this one?

Questions for the Third Pass

For the third pass of the talking piece, we suggested that participants consider the people in their lives whom they regard as their
personal "stars":

+ Who has been a star in your life—someone who has
guided you and lit your path?
+ How has this person affected your life?
+ What would your life likely have been like without this
person?
+ What wisdom has come into your life as a result of
your experiences with this person?

Thoughts for the Circle Closing

To close the Circle, we gave each participant a set of four holiday cards with stamped envelopes. We then invited the participants to meditate on the candle in the centerpiece and, as
they did, to think of four people who have been "stars" for them
in their lives. The cards were for them to send to these people,
if they wished. In the cards, the participants might share how
each person had helped them to see things about their lives
more clearly and how these insights had led them to make positive changes in their lives. We suggested that, although we were
going to put out the candle in the center, the light from their
stars would burn on, because they had a fixed place in their
hearts. We then invited one of the participants to extinguish
the flame.

Other Metaphors for Wisdom

Clowns

Throughout history and across cultures, clowns have taught us about wisdom by making us laugh at ourselves. They observe us acutely as we go through life's up and downs, and then they present caricatures of our expectations, fears, doubts, and weaknesses. Through playful antics, they lure us into accepting ourselves as we are and surrendering to life's inevitabilities. Clowns teach us not to take ourselves so seriously.

Not all clowns do this by making us laugh, though. Sad clowns project a gloomy mood or poignant situation. They hold up a mirror for us to see ourselves as we experience pain. Sad clowns don't reject the "silly clowns" who play right alongside them, suggesting that sadness and disappointment need not isolate us or steal our joy. Positive and negative emotions are part of the human condition, and happy and sad clowns communicate this truth.

With the wisdom we gain from clowns' performances, we learn to balance joy and sadness. Humor often causes us to shift our perspective on painful experiences, giving us a self-awareness—as well as insight, understanding, and compassion—that breaks through melancholy. From all clowns, we learn that the most healing wisdom often lies in the ability to laugh or cry without judgment.

For a centerpiece, we made a collage of images of clowns and clown dolls, and we used a clown finger puppet as the talking piece. To begin a round, we posed some questions:

+ What tends to make you laugh? What makes you sad?
+ How might the silly-wisdom of clowns help you balance the different emotions inside you?
+ What is something that you have noticed about your mental or emotional patterns or your behavior that you

find amusing—something that might make you laugh at yourself? What sort of silliness might you be caught up in, which may well coincide with whatever you find most heavy and least amusing?

+ What sort of happy or sad clown might you be, and what sort of caricatures of yourself might make you laugh?
+ Do you ever feel that happy and sad clowns live inside you? What sort of antics might they perform that would get your attention and help you see things differently?

A Magnifying Glass

A magnifying glass brings things into focus and makes them easier to see. It helps us clarify a message, read the fine print, or understand and complete a project more readily. Wisdom brings clarity as well, and it belongs in our emotional toolbox. Wisdom urges us to reflect on our lives: Who are we? What guides us? What is ours to do? According to wisdom, living life well involves regularly asking ourselves these core questions, because then we become more mindful of larger contexts and of how we fit in. Wisdom's "magnifying glass" provides a simple tool for introducing a clearer view of difficult situations. Without this tool, we could easily miss the deeper understandings that our experiences hold.

Using a large magnifying glass as the centerpiece and a small magnifying glass as the talking piece, we invited participants to use this metaphor for wisdom:

+ Do you agree that an unexamined life is a life unlived? Why might this be so?
+ What might be the benefit of examining your life?
+ How might you go about doing this?
+ What values would you bring to your self-examination?

+ If, on examining your life, you find things that you do not feel good about, what response might you have? How might you go about changing things?
+ If, on examining your life, you find things that you are happy about, how might this awareness help you? How might it affect your life and how you live it?

Maps and Compasses

Maps and compasses are navigational tools. Maps provide visual guides of a territory, while compasses direct our steps and keep us from getting disoriented or lost. Travelers, explorers, and adventurers of the past developed these tools so that those on journeys could find their way. Even if travelers had never been to a place before, with the help of these tools, they could arrive at their destination directly.

Wisdom as a value functions like a map and compass. Developed over time and through many experiences, wisdom gives us the perspective to make healthy choices and to avoid pitfalls. By following the map that hard-earned wisdom provides, we are better able to turn our lives in positive and productive directions.

Wisdom's map and compass are simple. We can reach a good destination (map) by practicing all the values—humility, patience, love, respect, integrity, courage, generosity, forgiveness, and gratitude—as our means for getting there (compass). Years of experiences have shown us what practicing good values means and what happens when we disregard them. As we check in with our best values, wisdom alerts us when we begin to lose sight of our values and drift into arrogant, impatient, disrespectful, ungenerous, or ungrateful patterns. Serving as a navigational tool through life, wisdom

> "The Circle experience has inspired me to begin making changes in my life that I have always feared."
>
> *–Circle participant incarcerated at the VOARCC*

keeps us on track with where we want to go and how we want to get there.

Using a packet of maps as the centerpiece and a compass as the talking piece, we invited participants to reflect on some goal that they were working toward in their future:

+ What is one goal that you would like to achieve over the next year?
+ What practical tools will you need to accomplish it?
+ What spiritual and emotional tools will you need?
+ How would examining your past help you attain your goal?
+ How might practicing values be important to your success? Correlatively, what might be the pitfalls if you did not practice certain values?

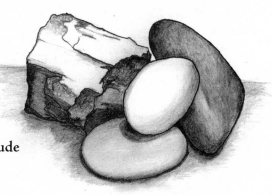

January

The Value of Fortitude

What is important to us will be challenged,
until we are one with it.

Deep in winter, January calls us to slow down, renew ourselves, affirm the year past, and anticipate the months to come. On New Year's Day, we make resolutions that require stamina and commitment, and we fortify ourselves with friendship, knowledge, and compassion to help us carry them out. As we practice our values, we realize that engaging any one value actually calls us to engage the others. Here with fortitude, to be strong, steadfast, and able to endure a long winter, we need humility, patience, love, and all the other values to see us through. The values help us structure another year of our lives in ways that will contribute to our character and growth. Practicing the different values shows us how to have fortitude—how to stand in the biting wind and not give up. The values together give us the means and wherewithal to endure.

In this sense, the value of fortitude is much like a stone shaped from a larger rock mass. The shape any stone possesses comes from its interactions with its environment—the worlds from which it came and through which it has journeyed. Water seeps into the tiny cracks of a cliff and then freezes and thaws, causing fissures. Plants grow in the cracks, and their roots divide the rock further. The cracks keep widening, until a chunk of rock detaches and falls away. The rock is then crushed and pounded by the ice, snow, wind, and rain. It rolls down hills and into streams, all the while being carved into its own distinct shape.

This pounding process is not unlike what we experience as we journey through change. To engage life is to be pounded, shaped, washed, broken, crushed, and carved. Fortitude tells us that when we feel this process going on, we have not failed or done something wrong, neither are we being punished by life. Quite the opposite: we are keenly alive, and we are simply facing another January of our life's cycle. Our transformation is at work, and fortitude is how we get through it—more, how we make the most of it by letting ourselves be changed. In January, then, we contemplate how our life processes might be like rocks and the forces that shape them. Our wintry experiences do not come to destroy us but to teach us strength in remaining true to our best selves and best values throughout life's upheavals and poundings.

What We Used for This Circle

- A bowl of stones with values engraved on them as the centerpiece
- Two rocks of similar shape, one heavier than the other, as the talking piece
- Closing gifts of the stones from the centerpiece

Thoughts for the Circle Opening

To open the Circle, we sent the two rocks that we were using as our talking piece around the Circle, and we invited the participants to place one rock in each hand and then to say her name out loud. We asked the participants to notice the weight of the rocks and how they chose to hold them. After the talking piece went around once and each participant had entered her name into the Circle, the two rocks came back to us.

Questions for the First Pass

Holding the two rocks, we pointed out that each participant had chosen one hand to hold the heavier rock and the other hand to hold the lighter rock. After making this observation, we framed the first round with some questions about that choice:

+ Why do you think the two rocks are different from each other in size and weight?
+ Which hand did you use to hold the heavy rock, and which hand did you use to hold the lighter one?
+ What did it feel like to hold the heavier rock?
+ What did you experience in holding the lighter rock?
+ Why do you think you were asked to say your name out loud?

Before passing the talking piece, we invited the participants to take a moment to reflect on holding the rocks and how they felt in each hand.

Questions for the Second Pass

Using their experiences with these two rocks as a metaphor to reflect on fortitude, we posed some more questions:

+ How might the practice of fortitude be reflected in your choice of which hand to use to hold each rock?
+ Can you recall a situation that you felt was too much for you to handle?
+ How did you respond to that situation?
+ What might a conscious intention to practice fortitude have looked like in that situation?
+ Without judging yourself for what you did or didn't

do, how might practicing fortitude have led you to deal
with that situation differently?

+ What might practicing fortitude have involved in that
situation? What would it have required of you?

Questions for the Third Pass

We invited the participants during the third pass to choose a
stone from the centerpiece bowl, and then we framed the third
round with another set of questions:

+ Why did you choose the stone that you did? What
might the stone symbolize for you?

+ Can you think of a person or situation in your life that
feels like an obstacle to you, making it more difficult for
you to attain your goals or keep your commitments?

+ How might practicing fortitude help you respond to
this situation?

+ What would practicing fortitude mean in this case?
What would it involve for you? Would you be able to
do it? If you're not sure, what might help you?

Thoughts for the Circle Closing

With the stones as closing gifts, we invited the participants to consider how they might embrace the value engraved on their stones
at a deeper level in their lives. How might fortitude help them
practice that particular value? We then shared some thoughts
about fortitude:

> Build a home in your heart for all that you value. When you
> experience pain and suffering, find your rock and hold on to
> it. Create a safe place—a place where you can fortify yourself
> with good values and relax the hardness in you, your defenses,

fears, and resistance—so that your strength and courage can emerge and keep you on a good path.

More Metaphors for Fortitude

A Compass and Map

Once again, each metaphor can be used in many ways. A magnetic compass, for example, suggests insights not only about wisdom but also about fortitude, since it always points north. It displays a constant point of reference, and we depend on its accuracy. A wise traveler would never go on a journey without one. With a compass in our pocket, we can take hikes or go on journeys with confidence, knowing that we can always find our way home. A compass gives us the means to "go the distance" and not get lost.

Like a compass, fortitude provides direction by keeping us oriented toward our values—our "north." With this constant point of reference, we can negotiate the complex terrain of our strengths, limits, and weaknesses, and thereby persevere in the face of obstacles. The busy-ness and chaos of life can easily leave us confused, tempting us to lose sight of our truth. Sometimes it takes a devastating loss to wake us up to how lost we have become. At those times, the way back depends on our ability to practice fortitude—our readiness to reorient our lives around our values and then to draw strength and courage from doing so.

Using a map as a centerpiece and a compass for the talking piece, we posed some questions for participants to consider:

+ What symbolizes your truth, your "north"?
+ How might you express your truth in a few words?
+ How do you use your truth to fortify yourself when you are in pain?

+ When you feel lost, how do you return to yourself?
  How does your truth serve as your compass? What
  brings you home?

A Hand Puppet

At a puppet show, the hand puppets lie limp until the puppe-
teers use their imagination and creativity to bring them to life.
The liveliness and personality of the toys depend on the hands
at work inside them. So, too, must we rely on what is inside of
us—our invisible reserves of strength and inspiration—to face
life's challenges. If what is inside us has been molded and shaped
by practicing values over many years, our inner reserves will
most likely be able to carry us through. If we need help, we know
healthy, value-affirming ways to get it.

Using a collection of hand puppets in a basket as the centerpiece and a single hand puppet as the talking piece, we raised
some questions to help participants focus on fortitude:

+ What is the inner core of your truth and strength?
+ What aspect of yourself do you depend on when times
  are tough?
+ How do you use your originality and inventiveness to
  fortify yourself?
+ Which person in your life supports you when you are
  in pain? How does that person help you at those times?

A Rattle

As with a hand puppet, what is inside a rattle enables it to serve
its purpose, namely, to make rattling sounds. A beautifully made
rattle without its inner workings would have no function, no
matter how much time may have been spent creating it. It is the
invisible inner dynamics that constitutes its existence as a rattle.

Applying the metaphor to human beings, we may focus our energies on creating an outer image that meets the expectations of families, cultures, or relationships but neglect to spend comparable time on developing our inner character. Yet it is only from the inside that our substance as a human being grows. If we spend time strengthening our inner core, we will develop the fortitude we need to respond well to whatever may come our way.

To push these two "inside" metaphors, fortitude is like our inner body, our bones and muscles. This inner body—our puppeteer or set of gourd seeds—gives us voice, motivating us and filling us with life and personality. We build our inner body through the nutrition and exercise we give to it. Standing by our values both when it is easy to do so and when it is difficult constitutes a powerful way to feed and exercise our inner body. Practicing fortitude in this way develops our strength, character, and resilience, so that we have the endurance to see us through not just the warm breezes of June but through January's cold winds as well.

Using a basket of rattles as the centerpiece and a single rattle as the talking piece, we invited participants to ponder:

+ How do you view your inner capacities and capabilities?
+ Do you consciously work on developing them? If so, how do you do this?
+ In what ways do you depend on yourself?
+ Who in your life supports you regardless of what you face?
+ What other values do you call on when you realize that you need to practice fortitude more intentionally and it is not proving easy?

February

The Value of Trust

> Trust is created moment to moment as we live
> our values.

In many parts of the country, February is still deep in the cold months. Spring can seem a long way off and waiting for the thaw can seem unending. Even so, we trust that winter will soon pass and spring will be here. In this sense, February is a waiting time, and when we wait, we have to trust that what we are waiting for will one day arrive. As far as the seasons go, this trust is warranted. The reliability and predictability of the changing seasons support our trust and enable us to make decisions accordingly. We have the assurance that spring will come.

With human beings, trust is more complex. We often don't know whom to trust or what to trust about someone. As we come to know people by observing their decisions and actions, though, we learn something about their natures. Whatever we can or cannot trust about others, we can trust that they will act from who they are, just as we will act from who we are. Each of us has weaknesses, shortcomings, family and cultural programming, fears, and doubts—"issues"—and these will show up in how we respond to experiences in regular, predictable ways. We also have knowledge and strengths derived from our experiences, and these will predictably shape our conduct and interactions as well. As we come to know people, we learn what we can trust about them. Equally, by knowing ourselves better, we learn what we can trust about ourselves too.

What is it, though, that we learn about people that then forms the basis of our decisions regarding trust? Up front, we learn their stories; we find out how they arrived at where they are—what their life's journey has included. In turn, as we share our life stories with others, we learn more about ourselves. By both hearing and telling story after story, we share experiences about our values—positive and negative. Based on these experiences, we sense which values are important to a person as well as to us. We also learn how we each go about living our values, since there are many ways to do this.

> "The feeling I experience in the Circle is a comforting presence. I want to foster that experience in my life and trust that, as I do, I will learn more about my responsibilities and my inner life. The Circle is a dynamic process that I seem to function well in."
>
> *—Circle participant incarcerated at the VOARCC*

For example, through one woman's story, we may sense that she approaches life in a sincere and humble way, and it may inspire us to reflect on the role that humility plays in our own lives. So, too, with all the other values we have explored: we listen for the values at work in people's experiences. When we see someone consistently practicing a value, we feel that we can trust the person to bring this value to his or her interactions with us as well. Similarly, when we notice ourselves placing a priority on a particular value, we learn to trust ourselves to act in ways consistent with it. Noticing the values at work in stories, lives, and experiences—our own and those of others—helps us decide whom we can trust and what we can trust. Can we trust this person to behave in a good way? Can we trust ourselves to do the same?

Building trust takes time and comes from years of experiences.

The capacities to trust and be trusted are precious gifts—qualities that we may strive to expand all our lives. Trustworthiness itself is an important value, and it is expressed in dependable actions and consistent follow-through.

What happens, then, when trust is broken? To break someone's trust or to have our trust broken is a painful and usually messy experience. It's so painful, in fact, that the temptation may be to recoil, pull back, and end the relationship, rather than slog through working things out. As understandable as this reaction may be, it carries a high price, both in what we lose and in what we fail to gain. Working to rebuild trust in a relationship involves going deeper into our values. It involves coming to terms with issues that we may have been avoiding, and it calls for consistency and steadfastness in our commitment to confronting issues and "making things right." Genuine amends are called for when trust is broken, and what needs to be done has to be worked out among all those involved.

> "I trusted in the Circle's process, and my trust paid off spiritually and practically. I became aware of how I had failed my family and lost their trust. As I make amends to my family, I trust that my future will be healthier and more fulfilled."
>
> —Circle participant incarcerated at the VOARCC

Mending broken trust is hard work that calls for our best values. Sincerely and diligently done, though, the process of rebuilding trust can eventually lead to deeper and more meaningful relationships. When trust is experienced, lost, and then rebuilt, a more solid foundation may develop, because we have to go through the experience of wrestling with what trust is all about—together.

What We Used for This Circle

- A basket of eggs for the centerpiece
- A raw egg for the talking piece

Thoughts for the Circle Opening

Trust can be compared to a raw egg: a lot went into its making, and a lot can be done with it, but to do anything, we need to handle the egg with care. If it breaks, the damage can be difficult to mend. The egg could represent, for example, a personal, private truth that we have chosen to share with another person. We trust that the person will, without reservation, do her best to protect the fragility and integrity of our truth. Being considered trustworthy is a significant human achievement, yet with that honor comes a significant responsibility.

Questions for the First Pass

Before passing the talking piece, we invited participants to share their thoughts about handling the egg when it came to them and suggested that everyone consciously trust that the egg would be passed to them without being broken or causing a mess. We then posed some questions about trust:

+ Why would you choose to trust someone?
+ Do you believe that you deserve the trust and respect of others? Why?
+ How does trust or the lack of trust impact one of your intimate relationships?
+ What have you done in the past when someone broke your trust?
+ What would you do if you were the one who broke someone's trust?

Questions for the Second Pass

+ How do you avoid creating messes in your personal relationships?

+ How might you be responsible for breaking the trust that someone has given you?
+ If someone broke your trust, what would you need to re-establish the relationship?

Questions for the Third Pass

Following the summary of the second pass, we invited the participants to hand the raw egg to the next person, once again trusting that each person would pass the egg with care and consideration. We then invited the participants to comment on another set of questions:

+ What did you experience when the raw egg was handed to you?
+ What enabled you to trust the participant who was passing you the egg?
+ What might "a raw egg" and "passing a raw egg" mean to you in your life and relationships?
+ Who in your personal life would you trust enough to "hand you a raw egg"?
+ Why would you trust that person?
+ Would you be trusted to pass someone in your life "a raw egg"?

Thoughts for the Circle Closing

We handed out pencils and oval-shaped pieces of paper and invited participants to write down their personal definition of trust and place it in front of them. We then passed the egg around the Circle again, giving each participant an opportunity to share her definition of trust.

More Metaphors for Trust

Road Signs

When navigating the highways, we trust that the road signs directing us over unfamiliar terrain are accurate indicators of what lies ahead. Road signs give us essential information: the speed limit, where to merge, when to stop, a dangerous curve ahead, the name of an intersecting road on an exit, the distances to different cities, and the location of rest areas and construction zones. Our lives literally depend on the accuracy of these signs, and we assume that we can trust them and follow them safely. If motorists lost trust in the posted road signs, the signs would be useless. In fact, even the highways would become virtually useless to travelers, because everyone except those who actually lived in an area would wander endlessly trying to find the right road or would become completely lost.

Like the trust we have in road signs, the trust we share with others is powerful and life-defining. Because trust is such an essential foundation of all human relations, breaking someone's trust or having our trust broken constitutes a profound betrayal, and it requires a serious and concerted effort to address whatever happened and work to regain trust.

Using some pictures of road signs as the centerpiece and a paper heart symbolizing the vulnerability implicit in trusting someone as the talking piece, we invited participants to reflect on some questions and, if they wanted, to share whatever thoughts came to their minds:

+ Over the course of your life, how have you learned about trust?
+ What have you learned?
+ How do you practice trust?
+ Why have you come to trust the people in your life?

+ Why do you think the people in your life have come to trust you?
+ On what do you base your decisions about who or what to trust and who or what not to trust?
+ What is the basis of your confidence in making these decisions? In other words, how do you know you are making good decisions? Do you have some standard or criterion to help you?

Lighthouses

Lighthouses function like road signs for boats. If mariners lacked confidence in the placement of lighthouses and in the reliability of their keepers (or, today, in their automated systems) to shine a light when necessary, they would not be able to navigate the waterways safely. Lighthouses perform a life-saving function, and mariners depend on them without reservation.

Likewise, we need to be able to trust our intimate relationships. Though we all go through changes that can alter us profoundly, our changeable natures do not make trust impossible. Trust develops in relationships over time, as we observe in each other how we each practice our values in different situations. We trust someone who, for example, seems consistently honest, open, compassionate, respectful, and understanding, and we are much less likely to trust someone who seems consistently or even occasionally dishonest, deceptive, judgmental, disrespectful, intrusive, controlling, or manipulative.

Trust operates similarly on a collective scale between peoples. When two peoples share a history of appropriate actions and fulfilled commitments, trust grows, just as trust is broken when a shared history reveals the opposite behavior. When trust is present, a sacred bond exists, and jeopardizing this bond in any way endangers good relations, whether the relation is between persons or between peoples.

Using a picture of a lighthouse as the centerpiece and a candle to symbolize the light and trust found in a relationship, we framed a Circle pass with some questions:

+ What enables you to trust another person?
+ How have you felt when your trust has been broken?
+ How do you feel when you break a trust?
+ If you were to break a trust, would you seek another chance to build trust with the person, and if you did, how and on what grounds?

The Sun

It is hard to imagine anything that we trust more than the rising and setting of the sun. What would happen if one day the sun didn't rise? We entrust much of the order and timing of our lives to the sun's existence. Indeed, life itself comes from the sun. All humanity depends on the cycles and predictability of the natural world, and we live with ease and confidence in knowing that the sun is predictable.

Like nature's cycles, extending trust and accepting it engage us in relationships that have a reliable and dependable quality. This does not mean, of course, that a relationship of mutual trust cannot shift, change, and move as we each journey through life. Neither does our commitment to being worthy of someone's trust commit us to fulfilling all the person's demands or expectations. Trust is not about binding us to one way of being or about one person controlling another. Instead, it is about balancing constancy and change. Looking at the natural world, the very reliability of natural cycles makes growth and change possible. Similarly, trust provides enough of a reliable basis in human relationships that personal change and movement become possible. To use the road sign and lighthouse metaphors, because we trust these signifiers to stay constant, we are able to move, change, and go forward.

Our centerpiece for this metaphor was a lamp to symbolize the sun's light and a vase of flowers to symbolize the sun's life-giving power. For the talking piece, we used a picture of the rising sun. We then invited participants to consider several questions about trust:

+ How is trust a life-affirming value?
+ In what sense might surrender be part of experiencing trust or giving it?
+ What risks do you take when you trust someone?
+ How can practicing trust be an antidote to fear, loneliness, or rejection?

Closing Thoughts:
Circles Belong to Their Participants

Writing this guide has given us an opportunity to underscore the role of values in the Circle process. In our experiences at the VOARCC, the discussion of values has been the backbone and essence of the Circles—what makes them so powerful. When values frame Circle dialogues, participants engage their capacities to develop relationships based on mutual understanding, compassion, and trust, and this experience is inevitably transforming.

Not that everyone agrees about things or sees life the same. Quite the opposite: Circle participants typically come from widely different backgrounds, peoples, cultures, and experiences. Yet the very power of Circles grows from their ability to "hold a space" where people can share diverse views in a safe and receptive atmosphere. Values provide the links for doing this. Because of the value-based nature of the process, Circles allow us to explore our differences in a good way—a way that can be mutually transforming.

> "Circles create a safe environment for healing to begin. Through our involvement in Circles, we have seen the seemingly impossible become possible."
>
> —Mark Clements, Circle of Harmony Team

For example, participants strive to say what they need to say, however difficult or painful it may be, with respect, humility, patience, and even love. The result is that participants learn how to share from the heart, discuss personal matters openly and honestly, and come to agreements through consent rather than coercion. This deepening of personal expression, even in the face of pain and conflicts, is a common Circle experience, and more often than not, it is life-changing.

In our VOARCC Circles, the participants embraced the Circle process largely because it gave them a chance to explore their values in ways they had never done before. They learned about themselves in relation to others, experienced the power of sharing and listening, and witnessed the transformative dynamics of value-centered discussions. They discovered that the more they organized their lives around values, the more they were positively motivated and found their relationships enriched.

Using metaphors to explore values was effective because it created a supportive framework in which participants could express what was most important to them. As participants shared their stories, we realized that clarifying our values had made it possible for us to reach common ground in how we wanted to express our individual truths to each other.

~ ~

We have shared with you some of our experiences of using metaphors to explore values in Circles. At first, you may choose to try out these same metaphors and questions in your own Circles. We naturally hope they are helpful. But we also want to emphasize, once again, that Circles are shaped by those involved, and the effectiveness of a Circle is connected to this shaping process—of participants working together. That being so, the ideal approach would be for participants to develop their own list of values as well as their own metaphors and questions for exploring them. The more participants engage in the process, the better and more effective the Circle will be.

This active participation is good for keepers, because it means the whole weight of choosing values and metaphors does not fall on them. In fact, the more keepers take the lead, the less the participants "buy into" the process. By contrast, when participants shape what goes on in Circles, they connect with what happens and open themselves to being transformed by it.

This being so, we want to emphasize that there are countless ways of bringing values into Circle dialogues, and we want to acknowledge Circle keepers for their continual efforts to create safe, meaningful spaces for discussing personal and shared truths. The role of Circle keepers requires sensitivity, openness, and flexibility. Our antennae need to be way out, and we need to be ready and willing to shift our approach at a moment's notice.

Recalling some of our own experiences, for example, we realized that sometimes a certain metaphor did not resonate with the Circle participants. When that happened, we had to adjust the process to respond to where the participants were mentally and emotionally. Sometimes we did a pass inviting the participants to suggest different metaphors for a particular value, or we suggested some different metaphors ourselves for the participants to consider. We also watched for pivotal moments in the Circle when we needed to honor the natural flow of the process as it developed, which we as keepers could not possibly predict. Sometimes the first pass of the talking piece raised issues that were so packed with potential for further discussion that we needed to do an additional pass or two to process all that had surfaced.

Given the many values that could be added to those in this guide and the countless metaphors that could shed light on these values, our hope is that this guide might serve simply as a starting point. We would like to close with a poem we wrote about our experiences with the women we came to know at the VOARCC:

> *Mystery unfolds at the birth of a child*
> *The flight of an eagle*
> *The emergence of a butterfly*
> *Embrace*
> *Wonder*
> *With each revelation*

Author and Illustrator Information

Pat Thalhuber is a Sister of Charity of the Blessed Virgin Mary (B.V.M.) from Dubuque, Iowa, now residing in Inver Grove Heights, Minnesota. Pat has found through her life as a teacher, youth coordinator, community programmer, and Circle keeper that empowering ideas and their implementation comes with heartfelt listening and a willingness to change. For more than a decade, she has initiated Circles in the community to address family and institutional needs. These Circles have been held within agencies as well as within the criminal justice system—e.g., at the VOARCC and the Juvenile Center in Hastings, Minnesota. She finds her most important education has come through her personal journey with those who witness by their lives that justice and peace are essential in forming right relations.

Susan Thompson lives in St. Paul, Minnesota, with her husband and daughter. She holds a Bachelor of Arts degree from the College of St. Catherine in St. Paul. She is grateful to all those she has met along the journey who have been teachers for her in their own ways. She spent one year training for Circles with the Circles of Harmony. She has also had the honor of taking part in the Circle training conducted by Phil Gatensby, who shared the wisdom of the elders from Yukon. She has been grateful to participate in Circles for twelve years and to keep Circles for eight years.

Pat and Susan are available to conduct workshops on value-centered Circles as well as to serve as Circle keepers. They invite

Circle keepers and participants to share with them how they have used the material in this book, especially how this guide may have inspired the exploration of other values, metaphors, and questions in a Circle context.

Loretta Draths has been on the staff of Living Justice Press since it started in 2002 and refers to her home as the press's "northern satellite office." She is also on staff at a sculpture park in Franconia, Minnesota. Her art training began with her mom in grade school and continues to this day. She has two wonderful children, Jake and Annie, who are now grown. She lives in Center City, Minnesota, with her husband, Fred, and Alice the cat.

Pat Thalhuber, Susan Thompson, and Loretta Draths may be contacted through:

Living Justice Press
Tel. (651) 695-1008 ✦ Fax. (651) 695-8564
2093 Juliet Avenue, St. Paul, MN 55105 USA
info@livingjusticepress.org ✦ www.livingjusticepress.org

About Living Justice Press

A nonprofit, tax-exempt publisher on restorative justice

Founded in 2002, Living Justice Press (LJP) is a 501(c)(3) non-profit organization whose purpose is to publish and promote alternative works about social justice and community healing. Our specific focus is on restorative justice and peacemaking, and within this field, our concentration is two-fold. First, we publish books that deepen the understanding and use of peacemaking Circles as a means not only to deal with conflict and harm but also to promote justice as a way of life. Second, we publish the voices of those "in struggle" for justice. Our books seek to apply what we have learned about healing harms between people to the larger challenge of addressing harms between Peoples. Through our publishing, we join in working toward justice between Peoples through paths of education, rectification, and transformation.

Our first two books—*Peacemaking Circles: From Crime to Community* by Kay Pranis, Barry Stuart, and Mark Wedge and *Justice As Healing: Indigenous Ways* edited by Wanda D. McCaslin—are being used extensively by tribal courts, tribal colleges, First Nations communities, law schools, universities, churches, law enforcement and probation departments, schools, youth centers, families, and, of course, community justice programs across the country and around the world.

Peacemaking Circles describes the philosophy and practice of the Circle process—a process that constitutes a major paradigm shift in how we respond to conflicts and harms. While one chapter is devoted to how the Circle process can be used in relation with the criminal justice system to create alternatives to incarceration or to support re-entry, the book as a whole has become a core text on the Circle process in general and how it can be used in many other contexts as well. It is currently being translated into Ukranian.

Justice As Healing presents a wide range of articles, mostly by Indigenous authors, about how conflicts can be used as opportunities for addressing deeper issues in relationships and how we can respond to these underlying problems in ways that heal people and strengthen communities. As many authors in this book explain, after suffering centuries of invasion, genocide, forced assimilation, and racism, Native communities are rebounding from the multigenerational trauma of this onslaught by drawing on their own traditions of community healing and peacemaking. The transformative power of this work is instructive and inspiring for both Native and non-Native audiences.

Our third book, *In the Footsteps of Our Ancestors: The Dakota Commemorative Marches of the 21st Century* edited by Waziyatawin Angela Wilson, deals with a longstanding, unaddressed, and largely unknown sequence of horrific harms between Peoples. Drawn from essays written by participants in the 2002 and 2004 Dakota Commemorative Marches, this book confronts the crimes of colonization, genocide, and forced removal perpetrated by Euro-Americans in Minnesota against the Dakota People, whose ancestral homeland Mni Sota Makoce is. It also explores what Dakota people are doing as a People to heal from this history and what White people can do as a People to work for justice today. A *St. Paul Pioneer Press* review stated that the lead article by Dr. Wilson "should be required reading in every school in the state [of Minnesota]." This brutal history is not at all unique to Minnesota, however, and the book's call to work toward justice between Peoples is compelling across the continent.

LJP's focus on the peacemaking Circle process has led to a series of books on this subject. *Building a Home for the Heart* serves as a companion volume to our first book, *Peacemaking Circles*, since discussing values is so central to the Circle process, no matter where or how it is used. We are soon to publish a third book in the peacemaking Circles series that focuses on how Circles are being used with youth. *Peacemaking Circles and Urban Youth: Bringing Justice Home* by Dr. Carolyn Boyes Watson discusses how the Circle process is being used by a remarkably innovative youth center in Chelsea, Massachusetts. Nearly twenty years in operation, Roca, Inc., works with immigrant, gang, and street youth in powerful and transformative ways, and using Circles extensively with youth and throughout the organization is integral to Roca's effectiveness. *Peacemaking Circles and Urban Youth* tells a compelling and inspiring story for any organization or person who works with youth.

We have several other books planned in our peacemaking Circle series. Several books currently in development focus on the use of peacemaking Circles in schools, while another describes how a community is using the Circle process in their local planning work, especially to deal with conflicts between different sectors in the community and their divergent interests.

In our series of books on working toward justice between Peoples, we look forward to publishing Gwen Chandler-Rhivers' powerful book, *Creating Space at the Table: Being Intentional About Antiracism in Restorative Justice*. Ms. Chandler-Rhivers is interviewing a number of People of Color working in the restorative justice movement about their insights and experiences around racism and effective antiracism, especially as it relates to the restorative justice work.

We are deeply grateful to those of you who have chosen to support us financially. Because publishing is so expensive, and because we try to keep the price of books as low as we can, we could not possibly make these books available without this support. For several years now, the Sisters of Charity of the Blessed

Virgin Mary (Dubuque, Iowa) and Yvonne Sexton of the Sexton Foundation (Saint Cloud, Minnesota) have given Living Justice Press generous grants that have enabled us to proceed with our publishing work. We are also most grateful to the Archie and Bertha H. Walker Foundation for their generous grant to us this past year. We have received generous support from individuals as well, including Jeannine Breton Baden, Mike Baden, Ernest J. Breton, Mary Joy Breton, Dave Buck, Clark Erickson, Sid Farrar, Deb Feeny, Barbara Gerten, Christopher Largent, Ruth Newman, Kay Pranis, Susan Sharpe, and Pat Thalhuber. One of our donors wishes to remain anonymous.

Thank you for the time and thought you have given to our publications. We appreciate your telling your family, friends, colleagues, and communities about our books, since that is how books get into the hands of those who want and need them. We invite you to add your name to our mailing list, so we can inform you of future books. We look forward to hearing from you, and we wish to express our gratitude to you for the thought and energies you give to justice and healing.

2093 Juliet Avenue, St. Paul, MN 55105
Tel. (651) 695-1008 • Fax. (651) 695-8564
E-mail: info@livingjusticepress.org
Web site: www.livingjusticepress.org

Index

Books from Living Justice Press

On the Circle Process and Its Uses

Peacemaking Circles: From Crime to Community by Kay Pranis, Barry
Stuart, and Mark Wedge, ISBN 0-9721886-0-6, paperback,
271 pages, index.

*Building a Home for the Heart: Using Metaphors in Value-Centered
Circles* by Pat Thalhuber, B.V.M., and Susan Thompson, foreword
by Kay Pranis, illustrated by Loretta Draths, ISBN 0-9721886-3-0,
paperback, 224 pages, index.

Peacemaking Circles and Urban Youth: Bringing Justice Home by Carolyn
Boyes Watson, ISBN 0-9721886-4-9, paperback, 290 pages
(approx.), index.

On Indigenous Justice

Justice As Healing: Indigenous Ways, edited by Wanda D. McCaslin,
ISBN 0-9721886-1-4, paperback, 459 pages, index.

On Addressing Harms between Peoples

*In the Footsteps of Our Ancestors: The Dakota Commemorative Marches
of the 21st Century*, edited by Waziyatawin Angela Wilson,
ISBN 0-9721886-2-2, oversize paperback, 316 pages, over
100 photographs, color photo insert, index.

We offer a 20% discount on orders of 10 books or more. We are de-
lighted to receive orders that come directly to us or through our Web
site. Our books are also available through amazon.com, and they can
be special ordered from most bookstores. Please check our Web site for
announcements of new LJP books.

Order by phone, fax, mail, or online at:
2093 Juliet Avenue, St. Paul, MN 55105
Tel. (651) 695-1008 ◆ Fax. (651) 695-8564
E-mail: info@livingjusticepress.org
Web site: www.livingjusticepress.org